Slow Cooking

the best cuisine is never rushed

Slow Cooking

the best cuisine is never rushed

Linda Doeser

BARNES
& NOBLE

NEW YORK

Original text by The Bridgewater Book Company
Re-edited by Linda Doeser
Photography by Karen Thomas, Mike Cooper and David Jordan
Designed by Talking Design

2006 Barnes & Noble Publishing

ISBN-13: 978-0-7607-8482-2
ISBN-10: 0-7607-8482-5

Printed and bound in China

1 3 5 7 9 10 8 6 4 2

Notes for the reader

This book uses imperial, metric, or US cup measurements. Follow the same units of measurements throughout, do not mix imperial and metric. All spoon measurements are level: teaspoons are assumed to be 5ml, and tablespoons are assumed to be 15ml. Unless otherwise stated, milk is assumed to be low fat and eggs are medium. The times given are an approximate guide only.

Some recipes contain nuts. If you are allergic to nuts you should avoid using them and any products containing nuts. Recipes using raw or very lightly cooked eggs should be avoided by infants, the elderly, pregnant women, convalescents, and anyone suffering from illness.

Contents

Life seems to grow more hectic by the day and there never seems to be enough time to do all the things we have to, let alone those we want to. We struggle to balance work and family commitments and now we are all being told to take more exercise and eat a healthier diet.

Introduction

The solution to the second part of this problem is the slow cooker. The idea is very simple—you put the ingredients in the cooker, switch it on (it's electric), then safely go to work, go shopping, take the kids to the game, do whatever you want to do, and some hours later, come home and you have a delicious meal waiting for you. The slow cooker cooks the food at a temperature high enough to ensure that microbes are destroyed and the ingredients become tender, but low enough to prevent liquid from evaporating and the food burning. This also means that if your meeting overruns or you're caught in traffic, your meal will not be spoiled. It will be ready when you are ready to eat it.

The hardware

The slow cooker consists of a base unit, which contains the heating element, and an inner ceramic cooking pot. In modern cookers, this pot is invariably removable but in some older models it is fixed. It is supplied with a lid, usually made of heatproof glass nowadays. This lets you check on progress without lifting it and so lowering the temperature inside the pot. The base unit may be encased in a heatproof material and its handles and the handle on the lid are very likely to be cool-touch. Note, however, that the inner pot will become very hot during cooking and you should always wear oven mitts when handling it. The base unit stands securely on two or more feet.

The cooker is usually controlled by a dial, although older models may simply have a switch. Typical dial positions are "off," "low," "high," and "auto". Some cookers also include "medium". The older switch controls are "low" and "high" but do not always include "off". Such cookers must, therefore, be switched off at the electrical socket.

The precise design of individual cookers varies and it is important that you read the manufacturer's instructions. These will give guidelines about using, cleaning, and storage of your particular model.

A variety of sizes is available to suit your individual needs, but remember that the base unit can mislead you into thinking that the cooking pot holds more than it really does. A 4-quart working capacity is suitable for most families and is not so large that it is difficult to find storage space. Round and oval cookers are produced and both have benefits and drawbacks.

What you can cook

The slow cooker is surprisingly versatile, although it cannot be used for every kind of cooking. There must be liquid of some sort in the cooker for it to function properly, so it is ideal for casseroles, stews, soups, and pasta sauces. You can also use it as a water bath for delicate foods, such as egg custards, which will work only if cooked slowly at a low temperature. It is invaluable for serving hot punch or mulled wine at a party, too. While it is perfect for pot roasts, it cannot be used for traditional roasts or, indeed, anything that is normally cooked at a high temperature in the oven, a skillet, or a deep-fryer, or under the broiler. Nor is it suitable for foods, such as pasta, that require vigorous boiling, as the temperature always remains below 212°F.

The slow cooker works as well for chicken casseroles as it does for vegetable curries and there are few ingredients that cannot be cooked this way. It is especially good for less tender cuts of meat, such as braising beef, and, as these are usually less expensive, it's good for the family budget as well. Long cooking at a low temperature tenderizes the meat, while at the same time, condensation on the inside of the lid forms a seal that keeps the meat succulent.

Vegetarian dishes and vegetable accompaniments also work well. However some, especially root vegetables, take a very long time to cook. For those used to the convention of cooking vegetables briefly in the minimum amount of liquid it can come of something of a shock when they first start using a slow cooker to look at the timing and amount of liquid. Be assured, however, that texture, color, flavor, and nutritional content will all be retained. On the other hand, cooking lentils and dried beans is simplicity itself—and there is no need to worry about the liquid boiling over or boiling dry.

You can use the slow cooker for fish and shellfish, but the technique is slightly different as they cannot withstand prolonged cooking and will lose their flavor and disintegrate. Use the slow cooker in the usual way for preparing the base of a stew or sauce with, for example, onion, tomatoes, and other vegetables, then add the fish or shellfish for the last part of the cooking time. They always need to be cooked on the high setting and take 30–60 minutes.

Using the slow cooker

No special preparation is required for meat, poultry, and vegetables and these may be sliced, diced, or chopped in the usual way. It is worth trimming off visible fat from any meat and, of course, this is healthier too. (You can also skim off any fat from the surface when the dish has finished cooking.) When preparing root vegetables, you may find it helpful to slice more thinly or chop more finely than you are used to when cooking on the stove or in the oven.

You can put all the ingredients straight into the slow cooker, add the liquid, and switch on. However, meat and poultry look more attractive and retain more flavor if they are lightly browned first. Some recipes in this book recommend tossing them in flour before browning. Similarly, onions and some other vegetables benefit from being lightly softened in a skillet with oil or melted butter for around 5 minutes before adding them to the cooker.

Mainly commonsense kitchen rules apply. Most dried legumes still need to be soaked before cooking and those that should be pre-boiled vigorously for 15 minutes—aduki, black, borlotti, and red kidney beans, and black-eyed peas—should still be treated this way. After pre-boiling, drain them well before adding to the slow cooker.

There are a few watch points when using a slow cooker. Frozen foods should always be thawed thoroughly before they are added. It has always been necessary to thaw meat and poultry before cooking, whatever the method, to safeguard health. With the slow cooker, even vegetables such as frozen peas must be thawed first. Otherwise they will dramatically lower the temperature of the cooker and the optimum temperature may not be regained, resulting in uncooked food and increased risk to health. It is also a good idea to remove ingredients that have been marinating in the refrigerator about 30 minutes before adding them to the slow cooker to let them return to room temperature. For a similar reason, it is usually advisable to bring the liquid to be added—stock, water, fruit juice, etc.—to boiling point before it is added to the cooker. This ensures that the optimum temperature is reached as quickly as possible. As a general rule, you will need slightly less liquid than required in recipes for conventional cooking because less will evaporate. Finally, it is best not to add dairy products, such as cream and yogurt, until the last 30 minutes of the cooking time to prevent them from curdling.

When you are ready to cook, place the slow cooker on a level counter and make sure that the cord does not hang over the edge. Check that the dial is on the "off" position before you plug the cooker into the socket. Remove the cooking pot from the base unit to avoid spilling ingredients and splashing liquid into the base when you are adding them. (This is not a concern with older models as the cooking pot is sealed to the base unit.)

Place the prepared ingredients in the cooking pot, but do not fill it more than about two-thirds full to allow room for expansion and for the heat to spread easily and evenly. Return the pot to the base unit, place the lid on top, and switch the cooker on. Cook on the setting specified in the recipe for the time suggested. Do not remove the lid during cooking, however tempting it is to prod around with a wooden spoon, because this will lower the temperature and it takes quite a long time for the cooker to return to the optimum. Stirring part of the way through the cooking time is recommended in a very few recipes and in some others, delicate ingredients, such as mushrooms and shrimp, are added toward the end of the cooking time. Try not to lift the lid during the first half of the cooking time, then stir or add at the appropriate time, and re-cover with the lid as soon as possible.

The cooking times in the recipes are guidelines and not precise. Many different things can cause a variation, from the thickness of vegetable slices to the freshness of dried legumes. As it's almost impossible to overcook a dish in the slow cooker, with the exception of fish and shellfish, this should not be a problem. As you get used to using it, you will acquire a "feel" for cooking times. Recipes state whether the setting should be high or low—the former cooks twice as quickly as the latter. As a general guide, soups, stews, and sauces are best cooked on low, while legumes, fish, and some vegetable dishes are best cooked on high. Manufacturers recommend that you do not leave the cooker completely unattended on the high setting as there is a slight risk of the liquid drying out. If you have to go out or you want to cook overnight, use the auto setting if you have one because the cooker starts cooking on the high setting and then switches to low.

Safety tips

• Make sure that the cooker is out of the reach of children and that the cord does not hang over the edge of the counter.
• Do not switch on the slow cooker without the cooking pot in position.
• Do not use the slow cooker if the cable, plug, base unit, cooking pot, or lid is damaged.
• Never put ingredients directly into the base of the slow cooker.
• Do not reheat food in the slow cooker.
• Make sure that food is cooked through before serving. This is especially important with meat products, pork, and poultry. Pierce the thickest part with the point of a sharp knife and if the juices show any traces of pink or red, continue to cook for a little longer. If the juices run clear, the meat is cooked through.
• Don't peer into the slow cooker when you first lift the lid as the steam that billows out might scald your face.
• Always use oven mitts when lifting out the cooking pot.

guide to recipe key

🍽️	SERVES 4	Guide to serving portions.
🥣	10 MINUTES	Preparation time.
🧤	10 MINUTES	Cooking time.

To Start

A great first course, this colorful country soup also makes a delicious light lunch served with a seeded bread.

Greek Bean & Vegetable Soup

Ingredients

2¾ cups dried navy beans,
   soaked in cold water overnight

2 onions, finely chopped

2 garlic cloves, finely chopped

2 potatoes, chopped

2 carrots, chopped

2 tomatoes, peeled and chopped

2 celery stalks, chopped

4 tbsp extra virgin olive oil

1 bay leaf

salt and pepper

To garnish

12 black olives

2 tbsp chopped fresh chives

Serves 4–6

Preparation time: 15 minutes,
plus overnight soaking

Cooking time: 12 hours

1. Drain the beans and rinse well under cold running water. Place them in the slow cooker and add the onions, garlic, potatoes, carrots, tomatoes, celery, olive oil, and bay leaf.

2. Pour in 8¾ cups boiling water, making sure that all the ingredients are fully submerged. Cover and cook on low for 12 hours until the beans are tender.

3. Remove and discard the bay leaf. Season the soup to taste with salt and pepper, and stir in the olives and chives. Ladle into warmed soup bowls and serve.

This is a two-for-the-price-of-one dish as you can serve the broth as a first course and serve the chicken for the main course.

Chicken & Leek Soup

Ingredients

12 prunes, pitted, or 12 no-soak prunes

4 chicken portions

4 cups sliced leeks

6¼ cups boiling chicken or beef stock

1 bouquet garni

salt and pepper

Serves 6–8

Preparation time: 15 minutes, plus 7 hours soaking

Cooking time: 7½ hours

---

1. If using fresh prunes, place them in a bowl and add cold water to cover. Let soak while the soup is cooking.

2. Place the chicken portions and leeks in the slow cooker. Pour in the stock and add the bouquet garni. Cover and cook on low for 7 hours.

3. If you are going to serve the chicken with the soup, remove it from the cooker with a slotted spoon and cut the meat off the bones. Cut it into bite-size pieces and return it to the cooker. Otherwise, leave the chicken portions in the slow cooker.

4. Drain the prunes, if necessary. Add the prunes to the soup and season to taste with salt and pepper. Re-cover and cook on high for 30 minutes.

5. Remove and discard the bouquet garni. Either ladle the soup, including the cut-up chicken, into warm bowls or remove the chicken portions and keep warm for the main course, then ladle the broth into warmed bowls. Serve immediately.

Bacon and lentils have a real affinity—their flavors and textures complement one another. This substantial soup also includes a selection of tasty winter vegetables.

Bacon & Lentil Soup

Ingredients

1 lb thick, rindless smoked bacon strips, diced

1 onion, chopped

2 carrots, sliced

2 celery stalks, chopped

1 turnip, chopped

1 large potato, chopped

⅓ cup green lentils

1 bouquet garni

4 cups chicken stock or water

salt and pepper

Serves 4

Preparation time: 15 minutes, plus 12–15 minutes pre-cooking

Cooking time: 8–9 hours

1. Heat a large, heavy pan. Add the bacon and cook over low heat, stirring frequently, for 4–5 minutes, until the fat runs. Add the onion, carrots, celery, turnip, and potato and cook, stirring frequently, for 5 minutes.

2. Add the lentils and bouquet garni and pour in the stock. Bring to a boil, then transfer the mixture to the slow cooker. Cover and cook on low for 8–9 hours, or until the lentils are tender.

3. Remove and discard the bouquet garni and season the soup to taste with pepper and salt, if necessary. Ladle into warmed soup bowls and serve.

Not only is this spicy, warm dip a tasty appetizer, but it is also an ideal party snack. Serve it with a selection of dippers if you like.

Tex-Mex Bean Dip

Ingredients

2 tbsp corn oil

1 onion, finely chopped

2 garlic cloves, finely chopped

2–3 fresh green chiles, seeded and finely chopped

14 oz canned refried beans or red kidney beans

2 tbsp chili sauce or taco sauce

6 tbsp hot vegetable stock

1 cup Cheddar cheese, grated

salt and pepper

1 fresh red chile, seeded and shredded, to garnish

tortilla chips, to serve

Serves 4

Preparation time: 15 minutes, plus 5 minutes pre-cooking

Cooking time: 2 hours

1. Heat the oil in a large, heavy skillet. Add the onion, garlic, and chiles and cook, stirring occasionally, over low heat for 5 minutes until the onion is soft and translucent. Transfer the mixture to the slow cooker.

2. Add the refried beans to the slow cooker. If using red kidney beans, drain well and rinse under cold running water. Reserve 2 tablespoons of the beans and mash the remainder coarsely with a potato masher. Add all the beans to the slow cooker.

3. Add the sauce, hot stock, and grated cheese, season with salt and pepper, and stir well. Cover and cook on low for 2 hours.

4. Transfer the dip to a serving bowl, garnish with shredded red chile, and serve warm with tortilla chips on the side.

An attractive vegetarian appetizer, this lightly spiced dish can also be served as an accompaniment to chicken or simply broiled fish.

Louisiana Zucchini

Ingredients

2 lb 4 oz zucchini, thickly sliced

1 onion, finely chopped

2 garlic cloves, finely chopped

2 red bell peppers, seeded and chopped

5 tbsp hot vegetable stock

4 tomatoes, peeled and chopped

2 tbsp butter, diced

salt and cayenne pepper

Serves 6

Preparation time: 15 minutes

Cooking time: 2½ hours

1. Place the zucchini, onion, garlic, and bell peppers in the slow cooker and season to taste with salt and cayenne pepper. Pour in the stock and mix well.

2. Sprinkle the chopped tomatoes on top and dot with the butter. Cover and cook on high for 2½ hours until tender.

Messy but delicious, chicken wings are also good to serve as party nibbles—just increase the quantity.

Sweet-and-Sour Chicken Wings

Ingredients
1 lb 4 oz chicken wings, tips removed
2 celery stalks, chopped
3 cups boiling chicken stock
2 tbsp cornstarch
3 tbsp white wine vinegar or rice vinegar
3 tbsp dark soy sauce
5 tbsp sweet chili sauce
¼ cup brown sugar
14 oz canned pineapple
    chunks in juice, drained

7 oz canned sliced bamboo
    shoots, drained and rinsed
½ green bell pepper, seeded and thinly
    sliced
½ red bell pepper, seeded and thinly sliced
salt

🍽 Serves 4–6

🥣 Preparation time: 10 minutes,
    plus 10 minutes for the sauce

🍲 Cooking time: 5 hours

1. Put the chicken wings and celery in the slow cooker and season with salt. Pour in the chicken stock, cover, and cook on low for 5 hours.

2. Drain the chicken wings, reserving 1½ cups of the stock, and keep warm. Pour the reserved stock into a pan and stir in the cornstarch. Add the vinegar, soy sauce, and chili sauce. Place over a medium heat and stir in the sugar. Cook, stirring constantly, for 5 minutes, or until the sugar has dissolved completely and the sauce is thickened and smooth.

3. Lower the heat, stir in the pineapple, bamboo shoots, and bell peppers and simmer gently for 2–3 minutes. Stir in the chicken wings until they are thoroughly coated, then transfer to a serving platter.

Garbanzos have a deliciously nutty flavor that works well with a herb dressing. They are notorious for taking ages to cook, so the slow cooker solves the problem.

Warm Garbanzo Bean Salad

Ingredients
1 cup dried garbanzo beans, soaked
   overnight in cold water and drained
1 cup pitted black olives
4 scallions, finely chopped
fresh parsley sprigs, to garnish
crusty bread, to serve

For the dressing
2 tbsp red wine vinegar
2 tbsp mixed chopped fresh herbs, such
   as parsley, rosemary, and thyme
3 garlic cloves, very finely chopped
½ cup extra virgin olive oil
salt and pepper

Serves 6

Preparation time: 10 minutes,
plus overnight soaking

Cooking time: 12 hours

1. Place the garbanzo beans in the slow cooker and add sufficient boiling water to cover. Cover and cook on low for 12 hours.

2. Drain well and transfer to a bowl. Stir in the olives and scallions.

3. To make the dressing, whisk together the vinegar, herbs, and garlic in a pitcher, and season with salt and pepper to taste. Gradually whisk in the olive oil. Pour the dressing over the still-warm garbanzos and toss lightly to coat. Garnish with the parsley sprigs and serve warm with crusty bread.

Served with a quick and easy sauce and a salad, these attractive molds make an unusual vegetarian main course or a substantial starter.

Eggplant Timbales

Ingredients
2 eggplants
3 tbsp olive oil, plus extra for greasing
2 onions, finely chopped
2 red bell peppers, seeded and chopped
1 large tomato, peeled and chopped
6 tbsp milk
2 egg yolks
pinch of ground cinnamon
1 cup finely crushed bread crumbs
salt and pepper
fresh cilantro sprigs, to garnish

For the sauce
1¼ cups sour cream
3–4 tbsp sun-dried tomato paste (optional)

Serves 4

Preparation time: 15 minutes, plus 20–25 minutes pre-cooking

Cooking time: 2 hours

1. Halve the eggplants and scoop out the flesh with a spoon. Reserve the shells and dice the flesh. Heat the oil in a large, heavy skillet. Add the onions and cook over low heat, stirring occasionally, for 5 minutes. Add the diced eggplant, bell peppers, and tomato and cook, stirring occasionally, for 15–20 minutes until all the vegetables are soft. Remove the skillet from the heat.

2. Transfer the mixture to a food processor or blender and process to a purée, then scrape into a bowl. Beat together the milk, egg yolks, cinnamon, and salt and pepper in a pitcher, then stir into the vegetable purée.

3. Brush 4 ramekins or cups with oil and sprinkle with the bread crumbs to coat. Tip out any excess. Mix about three-quarters of the remaining crumbs into the vegetable purée. Slice the eggplant shells into strips and use them to line the ramekins, leaving the ends protruding above the rims. Spoon the filling into the ramekins, sprinkle with the remaining crumbs, and fold the overlapping ends over.

4. Cover with foil and place in the slow cooker. Pour in sufficient boiling water to come about one-third of the way up the sides of the ramekins. Cover and cook on high for 2 hours.

5. To make the sauce, lightly beat the sour cream and add the tomato paste to taste, if desired. Season with salt and pepper. Lift the ramekins out of the cooker and remove the foil. Invert onto serving plates and serve with the sauce, garnished with cilantro sprigs.

This traditional New England dish can be served on its own with plenty of warm, fresh bread or as an accompaniment to roast pork.

Boston Baked Beans

Ingredients

2½ cups dried white haricot beans, soaked
  overnight in cold water and drained
4 oz salt pork, soaked in cold water for
  3 hours and drained
3 tbsp molasses
3 tbsp dark brown sugar
2 tsp dry mustard
1 onion, chopped
salt and pepper

Serves 4–6

Preparation time: 15 minutes,
plus overnight soaking

Cooking time: 3 + 11 hours
(14 hours in total)

1. Place the beans in the slow cooker and add about 6¼ cups boiling water so that they are covered. Cover and cook on high for 3 hours. Meanwhile, cut the salt pork into chunks.

2. Drain the beans, reserving 1 cup of the cooking liquid. Mix the reserved liquid with the molasses, sugar, mustard, and 1 teaspoon salt.

3. Return the beans to the slow cooker and add the salt pork, onion, and the molasses mixture. Stir, then cover, and cook on low for 11 hours.

4. Adjust the seasoning and serve immediately.

These tasty stuffed cabbage rolls make a great vegetarian appetizer but can also be served as a main course.

Cabbage Roulades with Tomato Sauce

Ingredients

1 cup mixed nuts, finely ground
2 onions, finely chopped
1 garlic clove, finely chopped
2 celery stalks, finely chopped
1 cup grated Cheddar cheese
1 tsp finely chopped thyme
2 eggs
1 tsp yeast extract
12 large green cabbage leaves

Tomato sauce

2 tbsp sunflower oil
2 onions, chopped

2 garlic cloves, finely chopped
1 lb 5 oz canned
    chopped tomatoes
2 tbsp tomato paste
1½ tsp sugar
1 bay leaf
salt and pepper

Serves 6

Preparation time: 25 minutes, plus 20 minutes pre-cooking

Cooking time: 3–4 hours

1. First make the tomato sauce. Heat the oil in a heavy pan. Add the onions and cook over medium heat, stirring occasionally, for 5 minutes until softened. Stir in the garlic and cook for 1 minute, then add the tomatoes, tomato paste, sugar, and bay leaf. Season with salt and pepper and bring to a boil. Lower the heat and simmer gently for 20 minutes until thickened.

2. Meanwhile, combine the nuts, onions, garlic, celery, cheese, and thyme in a bowl. Lightly beat the eggs with the yeast extract in a pitcher, then stir into the nut mixture. Set aside.

3. Cut out the thick stalk from the cabbage leaves. Blanch the leaves in a large pan of boiling water for 5 minutes, then drain, and refresh under cold water. Pat dry with paper towels.

4. Place a little of the nut mixture on the stalk end of each cabbage leaf. Fold the sides over, then roll up to make a neat packet.

5. Arrange the packets in the slow cooker, seam side down. Remove and discard the bay leaf from the tomato sauce and pour the sauce over the cabbage rolls. Cover and cook on low for 3–4 hours. Serve the cabbage roulades hot or cold.

Everyday Meals

Nothing is nicer on a cold winter evening than sitting down to this hearty, one-pot dish.

Chicken Stew

Ingredients

3 tbsp corn oil

1 large onion, thinly sliced

1 green bell pepper, seeded and chopped

8 chicken pieces, such as thighs
   and drumsticks

14 oz canned chopped tomatoes, drained

pinch of cayenne pepper

1 tbsp Worcestershire sauce

1¼ cups boiling chicken stock

1 tbsp cornstarch

generous 1 cup frozen corn, thawed

generous 3 cups frozen fava beans, thawed

salt

crusty bread, to serve

Serves 4

Preparation time: 20 minutes,
plus 10 minutes pre-cooking

Cooking time: 7 hours

---

1. Heat the oil in a large, heavy skillet. Add the onion and bell pepper and cook over medium heat, stirring occasionally, for 5 minutes until the onion is softened. Using a slotted spoon, transfer the mixture to the slow cooker.

2. Add the chicken to the skillet and cook, turning occasionally, for 5 minutes until golden all over. Transfer to the slow cooker and add the tomatoes. Season with a pinch of cayenne pepper and salt. Stir the Worcestershire sauce into the hot stock and pour into the slow cooker. Cover and cook on low for 6½ hours.

3. Mix the cornstarch to a paste with 2–3 tablespoons water and stir into the stew. Add the corn and beans, re-cover, and cook on high for 30–40 minutes until everything is cooked through and piping hot. Transfer to warm plates and serve with crusty bread.

This is a classic combination that is traditionally served in the winter when red cabbage is in season.

Chicken Braised with Red Cabbage

Ingredients

2 tbsp sunflower oil

4 skinless chicken thighs or drumsticks

1 onion, chopped

5½ cups shredded red cabbage

2 apples, peeled and chopped

12 canned or cooked chestnuts,
    halved (optional)

½ tsp juniper berries

½ cup red wine

salt and pepper

fresh flat-leaf parsley, to garnish

Serves 4

Preparation time: 15 minutes,
plus 10 minutes pre-cooking

Cooking time: 5 hours

1. Heat the oil in a large, heavy pan. Add the chicken and cook, turning frequently, for 5 minutes until golden on all sides. Using a slotted spoon transfer to a plate lined with paper towels.

2. Add the onion to the pan and cook over medium heat, stirring occasionally, until softened. Stir in the cabbage and the apples and cook, stirring occasionally, for 5 minutes. Add the chestnuts, if using, juniper berries, and wine and season to taste with salt and pepper. Bring to a boil.

3. Spoon half the cabbage mixture into the slow cooker, add the chicken pieces, then top with the remaining cabbage mixture. Cover and cook on low for 5 hours until the chicken is tender and cooked through. Serve immediately, garnished with the parsley.

This colorful dish is perfect for a family dinner in the early spring, when the days are growing longer but the evenings are still cool. Serve with plain boiled rice or crusty bread.

Chicken with Red Bell Pepper & Fava Beans

Ingredients

1½ tbsp all-purpose flour

4 chicken portions, about 6 oz each

2 tbsp olive oil

1 onion, chopped

2–3 garlic cloves, chopped

1 fresh red chile, seeded and chopped

8 oz chorizo or other spicy sausages,
    skinned and cut into small chunks

1¼ cups chicken stock

⅔ cup dry white wine

1 tbsp dark soy sauce

1 large red bell pepper, seeded and sliced
    into rings

1⅔ cups shelled fava beans

¼ cup arugula or baby spinach leaves

salt and pepper

🍽 Serves 4

Preparation time: 20 minutes,
plus 20 minutes pre-cooking

Cooking time: 7¼–7½ hours

---

1. Spread out the flour on a plate and season well with salt and pepper. Toss the chicken in the flour until thoroughly coated, shaking off any excess. Reserve any remaining flour.

2. Heat half the oil in a heavy skillet, add the chicken portions, and cook over medium–high heat, turning frequently, for 10 minutes, or until golden brown all over. Add a little more oil during cooking if necessary. Using a slotted spoon, transfer the chicken to the slow cooker.

3. Add the remaining oil to the skillet. Add the onion, garlic, and chile and cook over low heat, stirring occasionally, for 5 minutes, until softened. Add the chorizo and cook, stirring frequently, for a further 2 minutes. Sprinkle in the remaining flour and cook, stirring constantly, for 2 minutes, then remove the skillet from the heat. Gradually stir in the stock, wine, and soy sauce, then return the skillet to the heat, and bring to a boil, stirring constantly. Pour the onion mixture over the chicken, then cover and cook on low for 6½ hours.

4. Add the red bell pepper and beans to the slow cooker, re-cover, and cook on high for 45–60 minutes, until the chicken and vegetables are cooked through and tender. Season to taste with salt and pepper, stir in the arugula, and let stand for 2 minutes, until just wilted, then serve.

This unusual combination of flavors is a great way to perk up chicken portions without taking up much time or blowing the household budget. Caramelized apple slices add a special touch.

Chicken & Apple Pot

Ingredients

1 tbsp olive oil

4 chicken portions, about 6 oz each

1 onion, chopped

2 celery stalks, coarsely chopped

1½ tbsp all-purpose flour

1¼ cups clear apple juice

⅔ cup chicken stock

1 cooking apple, cored and cut into fourths

2 bay leaves

1–2 tsp honey

1 yellow bell pepper, seeded and
  cut into chunks

salt and pepper

For the garnish

1 tbsp butter, melted

1 large or 2 medium eating apples, cored
  and sliced

2 tbsp raw brown sugar

1 tbsp chopped fresh mint

Serves 4

Preparation time: 15 minutes,
plus 20 minutes pre-cooking

Cooking time: 7¼ hours

---

1. Heat the oil in a heavy skillet. Add the chicken and cook over medium–high heat, turning frequently, for 10 minutes, until golden brown all over. Using a slotted spoon, transfer the chicken to the slow cooker.

2. Add the onion and celery to the skillet and cook over low heat, stirring occasionally, for 5 minutes, until softened. Sprinkle in the flour and cook, stirring constantly, for 2 minutes, then remove the skillet from the heat. Gradually stir in the apple juice and stock, then return the skillet to the heat, and bring to a boil, stirring constantly. Stir in the cooking apple, bay leaves, and honey, and season to taste with salt and pepper.

3. Pour the mixture over the chicken, cover and cook on low for 6½ hours, until the chicken is tender and the juices run clear when the thickest part is pierced with the point of a sharp knife. Stir in the yellow bell pepper, re-cover, and cook on high for 45 minutes.

4. Shortly before you are ready to serve, preheat the broiler. Brush one side of the apple slices with half the melted butter and sprinkle them with half the sugar. Broil for 2–3 minutes, until the sugar has caramelized. Turn the slices over with tongs, brush with the remaining butter, and sprinkle with the remaining sugar. Broil for a further 2 minutes. Serve the stew garnished with the caramelized apple slices and the mint.

This traditional European dish partners chicken and mushrooms with red wine, the wine giving the onions in particular a delicious, rich flavor.

Chicken & Mushroom Stew

Ingredients

1 tbsp butter

2 tbsp olive oil

4 lb skinless chicken portions

2 red onions, sliced

2 garlic cloves, finely chopped

14 oz canned chopped tomatoes

2 tbsp chopped fresh flat-leaf parsley

6 fresh basil leaves, torn

1 tbsp sun-dried tomato paste

⅔ cup red wine

3¼ cups sliced mushrooms

salt and pepper

Serves 4

Preparation time: 10 minutes, plus 25 minutes pre-cooking

Cooking time: 7 hours

---

1. Heat the butter and oil in a heavy skillet. Add the chicken, in batches if necessary, and cook over medium–high heat, turning frequently, for 10 minutes, until golden brown all over. Using a slotted spoon, transfer the chicken to the slow cooker.

2. Add the onions and garlic to the skillet and cook over low heat, stirring occasionally, for 10 minutes, until golden. Add the tomatoes with their can juices, stir in the parsley, basil, tomato paste, and wine, and season with salt and pepper. Bring to a boil, then pour the mixture over the chicken.

3. Cover the slow cooker and cook on low for 6½ hours. Stir in the mushrooms, re-cover, and cook on high for 30 minutes, until the chicken is tender and the vegetables are cooked through. Taste and adjust the seasoning if necessary and serve.

Warming spices give this rich dish a delicious and unusual flavor that is sure to please a hungry family on a cold winter day.

Thick Beef & Pearl Onion Casserole

Ingredients

2 tbsp olive oil

1 lb pearl onions, peeled but left whole

2 garlic cloves, halved

2 lb braising beef, cubed

½ tsp ground cinnamon

1 tsp ground cloves

1 tsp ground cumin

2 tbsp tomato paste

3 cups red wine

grated rind and juice of 1 orange

1 bay leaf

salt and pepper

1 tbsp chopped fresh flat-leaf parsley, to garnish

boiled potatoes, to serve

Serves 6

Preparation time: 20 minutes, plus 15 minutes pre-cooking

Cooking time: 9 hours

---

1. Heat the oil in a heavy skillet. Add the onions and garlic and cook over medium heat, stirring frequently, for 5 minutes, until softened and beginning to brown. Increase the heat to high, add the beef, and cook, stirring frequently, for 5 minutes, until browned all over.

2. Stir in the cinnamon, cloves, cumin, and tomato paste, and season with salt and pepper. Pour in the wine, scraping up any sediment from the base of the skillet. Stir in the orange rind and juice, add the bay leaf, and bring to a boil.

3. Transfer the mixture to the slow cooker, cover and cook on low for 9 hours, until the beef is tender. If possible, stir the stew once during the second half of the cooking time.

4. Serve the stew garnished with the parsley and accompanied by boiled potatoes.

This is an ideal dish for busy people as it contains everything you need for a filling and healthy meal, so there is no need to prepare any accompaniments.

Beef & Vegetable Stew with Corn

Ingredients

1½ tbsp all-purpose flour

1 tsp hot paprika

1–1½ tsp chili powder

1 tsp ground ginger

1 lb braising beef, cubed

2 tbsp olive oil

1 large onion, cut into chunks

3 garlic cloves, sliced

2 celery stalks, sliced

1¼ cups chopped carrots

1¼ cups lager

1¼ cups beef stock

1¼ cups chopped potatoes

2 corn cobs, halved

1 red bell pepper, seeded and chopped

4 oz tomatoes, cut into fourths

½ cup shelled peas, thawed if frozen

1 tbsp chopped fresh cilantro

salt and pepper

Serves 4

Preparation time: 20 minutes, plus 12 minutes pre-cooking

Cooking time: 9¼ hours

---

1. Combine the flour, paprika, chili powder and ginger in a shallow dish, add the steak cubes, and toss well to coat. Shake off any excess.

2. Heat the oil in a heavy skillet. Add the onion, garlic, and celery and cook over low heat, stirring occasionally, for 5 minutes, until softened. Increase the heat to high, add the steak, and cook, stirring frequently, for 3 minutes, until browned all over. Add the carrots and remove the skillet from the heat.

3. Gradually stir in the lager and stock, return the skillet to the heat, and bring to a boil, stirring constantly. Transfer the mixture to the slow cooker, add the potatoes and corn cobs, cover, and cook on low for 8½ hours.

4. Add the bell pepper, tomatoes, and peas, re-cover and cook on high for 45 minutes, until the meat is tender and the vegetables are cooked through. Taste and adjust the seasoning if necessary, sprinkle with the cilantro, and serve.

This dish originated in Provence in the south of France where it is usually served with buttered noodles. It is equally good with a mound of hot mashed potatoes.

Beef Stew with Olives

Ingredients

2 lb braising beef, cubed

2 onions, thinly sliced

2 carrots, sliced

4 large garlic cloves, lightly crushed

1 bouquet garni

4 juniper berries

2¼ cups dry red wine

2 tbsp brandy

2 tbsp olive oil

3 tbsp all-purpose flour

⅔ cup lardons or diced bacon

2 x 4-inch strips of thinly pared orange rind

¾ cup pitted black olives, rinsed

salt and pepper

buttered noodles or tagliatelle, to serve

To garnish

1 tbsp chopped fresh flat-leaf parsley

finely grated orange rind

Serves 4–6

Preparation time: 20 minutes, plus 24 hours marinating

Cooking time: 9½–10 hours

---

1. Put the stewing steak in a large, nonmetallic dish, add the onions, carrots, garlic, bouquet garni, and juniper berries, and season with salt and pepper. Combine the wine, brandy, and olive oil in a pitcher and pour the mixture over the meat and vegetables. Cover with plastic wrap and marinate in the refrigerator for 24 hours.

2. Using a slotted spoon remove the steak from the marinade and pat dry with paper towels. Reserve the marinade, vegetables, and flavorings. Place the flour in a shallow dish and season well with salt and pepper. Toss the steak cubes in the flour until well coated and shake off any excess.

3. Sprinkle half the lardons in the base of the slow cooker and top with the steak cubes. Pour in the marinade, including the vegetables and flavorings, and add the strips of orange rind and the olives. Top with the remaining lardons. Cover and cook on low for 9½–10 hours, until the steak and vegetables are tender.

4. Remove and discard the bouquet garni and skim off any fat that has risen to the surface of the stew. Sprinkle the parsley and grated rind over the top and serve with buttered noodles or tagliatelle.

There are many versions of this traditional beef stew, which dates back to the ninth century. Finishing it with sour cream is, however, a modern addition.

Goulash

Ingredients

4 tbsp sunflower oil

1 lb 7 oz braising beef, cut into 1-inch cubes

2 tsp all-purpose flour

2 tsp paprika

1½ cups beef stock

3 onions, chopped

4 carrots, diced

1 large potato or 2 medium potatoes, diced

1 bay leaf

½–1 tsp caraway seeds

14 oz canned chopped tomatoes

2 tbsp sour cream

salt and pepper

🍽 Serves 4

🥣 Preparation time: 20 minutes, plus 25 minutes pre-cooking

🧤 Cooking time: 9 hours

---

1. Heat half the oil in a heavy skillet. Add the beef and cook over medium heat, stirring frequently, until browned all over. Lower the heat and stir in the flour and paprika. Cook, stirring constantly, for 2 minutes. Gradually stir in the stock and bring to a boil, then transfer the mixture to the slow cooker.

2. Rinse out the skillet and heat the remaining oil in it. Add the onions and cook over low heat, stirring occasionally, for 5 minutes until softened. Stir in the carrots and potato and cook for a few minutes more. Add the bay leaf, caraway seeds, and tomatoes with their can juices. Season with salt and pepper.

3. Transfer the vegetable mixture to the slow cooker, stir well, then cover, and cook on low for 9 hours until the meat is tender.

4. Remove and discard the bay leaf. Pour over the sour cream and serve immediately.

Bring a hint of exotic North African cooking to the dinner table with this subtly spiced, succulent lamb stew flavored with orange juice.

Lamb Stew with Red Bell Peppers

Ingredients

1½ tbsp all-purpose flour

1 tsp ground cloves

1 lb boneless lamb, cut into thin strips

1–1½ tbsp olive oil

1 white onion, sliced

2–3 garlic cloves, sliced

1¼ cups orange juice

⅔ cup lamb or chicken stock

1 cinnamon stick

2 red bell peppers, seeded and
    sliced into rings

4 tomatoes

4 fresh cilantro sprigs

salt and pepper

1 tbsp chopped fresh cilantro, to garnish

To serve

mashed sweet potatoes mixed with
    chopped scallions

green vegetables

Serves 4

Preparation time: 15 minutes,
plus 15 minutes pre-cooking

Cooking time: 7–8 hours

---

1. Combine the flour and ground cloves in a shallow dish, add the strips of lamb, and toss well to coat, shaking off any excess. Reserve the remaining spiced flour.

2. Heat 1 tbsp of the oil in a heavy skillet, add the lamb, and cook over high heat, stirring frequently, for 3 minutes, until browned all over. Using a slotted spoon, transfer the lamb to the slow cooker.

3. Add the onion and garlic to the skillet, with the remaining oil if necessary, and cook over low heat, stirring occasionally, for 5 minutes, until softened. Sprinkle in the reserved spiced flour and cook, stirring constantly, for 2 minutes, then remove the skillet from the heat. Gradually stir in the orange juice and stock, then return the skillet to the heat, and bring to a boil, stirring constantly.

4. Pour the mixture over the lamb, add the cinnamon stick, bell peppers, tomatoes, and cilantro sprigs, and stir well. Cover and cook on low for 7–8 hours, until the meat is tender.

5. Remove and discard the cinnamon stick and cilantro sprigs. Season to taste with salt and pepper, sprinkle the stew with chopped cilantro, and serve with mashed sweet potatoes with scallions and green vegetables.

It is worth spending the extra dollars on country-cured ham from Virginia, Kentucky, Georgia, or Tennessee for this country-style dish as the flavor is indescribably superior.

Ham with Black-Eyed Peas

Ingredients

1 lb 4 oz country-cured ham
2–3 tbsp olive oil
1 onion, chopped
2–3 garlic cloves, chopped
2 celery stalks, chopped
6 oz carrots, thinly sliced
1 cinnamon stick
½ tsp ground cloves
¼ tsp freshly grated nutmeg
1 tsp dried oregano
2 cups chicken or vegetable stock
2 tbsp maple syrup
8 oz chorizo or other spicy sausages, skinned

14 oz canned black-eyed peas, drained and rinsed
1 orange bell pepper, seeded and chopped
1 tbsp cornstarch
pepper
fresh flat-leaf parsley or oregano sprig, to garnish

Serves 4

Preparation time: 20 minutes, plus 15 minutes pre-cooking

Cooking time: 6¼–7¾ hours

---

1. Trim off any fat from the ham and cut the flesh into 1½-inch pieces. Heat 1 tbsp of the oil in a heavy skillet, add the ham, and cook over high heat, stirring frequently, for 5 minutes, until browned all over. Using a slotted spoon, transfer the ham to the slow cooker.

2. Add 1 tbsp of the remaining oil to the skillet. Reduce the heat to low, add the onion, garlic, celery, and carrots, and cook, stirring occasionally, for 5 minutes, until softened. Add the cinnamon, cloves, and nutmeg, season with pepper, and cook, stirring constantly, for 2 minutes. Stir in the dried oregano, stock, and maple syrup and bring to a boil, stirring constantly. Pour the mixture over the ham, stir well, cover, and cook on low for 5–6 hours.

3. Heat the remaining oil in a skillet, add the chorizo, and cook, turning frequently, for 10 minutes, until browned all over. Remove from the skillet, cut each into 3–4 chunks, and add to the slow cooker with the black-eyed peas and bell pepper. Re-cover and cook on high for 1–1½ hours.

4. Stir the cornstarch with 2 tbsp water to a smooth paste in a small bowl, then stir into the stew, re-cover, and cook on high for 15 minutes. Remove and discard the cinnamon stick, garnish the stew with a fresh herb sprig, and serve.

This lovely summery dish is perfect for family suppers and is special enough to serve to guests.

Tagliatelle with Shrimp

Ingredients

14 oz tomatoes, peeled and chopped

5 oz tomato paste

1 garlic clove, finely chopped

2 tbsp chopped fresh parsley

1 lb 2 oz cooked, peeled large shrimp

6 fresh basil leaves, torn

14 oz dried tagliatelle

salt and pepper

fresh basil leaves, to garnish

 Serves 4

Preparation time: 5 minutes

Cooking time: 7¼ hours

1. Put the tomatoes, tomato paste, garlic, and parsley in the slow cooker and season with salt and pepper. Cover and cook on low for 7 hours.

2. Add the shrimp and basil. Re-cover and cook on high for 15 minutes.

3. Meanwhile, bring a large pan of lightly salted water to a boil. Add the pasta, bring back to a boil, and cook for 10–12 minutes until tender but still firm to the bite.

4. Drain the pasta and tip it into a warm serving bowl. Add the shrimp sauce and toss lightly with 2 large forks. Garnish with the basil leaves and serve immediately.

This famous southern stew gets its name from the West African name for okra-gumbo—a vegetable that not only provides flavor but helps to thicken it.

Louisiana Gumbo

Ingredients

2 tbsp sunflower or corn oil

6 oz okra, trimmed and cut into
  1-inch pieces

2 onions, finely chopped

4 celery stalks, very finely chopped

1 garlic clove, finely chopped

2 tbsp all-purpose flour

½ tsp sugar

1 tsp ground cumin

3 cups fish stock

1 red bell pepper, seeded and chopped

1 green bell pepper, seeded and chopped

2 large tomatoes, chopped

4 tbsp chopped fresh parsley

1 tbsp chopped fresh cilantro

dash of Tabasco

12 oz jumbo shrimp, peeled and deveined

12 oz cod or haddock fillet, skinned and
  cut into 1-inch chunks

12 oz monkfish fillet, cut into 1-inch chunks

salt and pepper

Serves 6

Preparation time: 30 minutes,
plus 15 minutes pre-cooking

Cooking time: 5½–6½ hours

1. Heat half the oil in a heavy skillet. Add the okra and cook over low heat, stirring frequently, for 5 minutes, until browned. Using a slotted spoon, transfer the okra to the slow cooker.

2. Add the remaining oil to the skillet. Add the onions and celery, and cook over low heat, stirring occasionally, for 5 minutes, until softened. Add the garlic and cook, stirring frequently, for 1 minute, then sprinkle in the flour, sugar, and cumin, and season with salt and pepper. Cook, stirring constantly for 2 minutes, then remove the skillet from the heat.

3. Gradually stir in the stock, then return the skillet to the heat, and bring to a boil, stirring constantly. Pour the mixture over the okra and stir in the bell peppers and tomatoes. Cover and cook on low for 5–6 hours.

4. Stir in the parsley, cilantro, and Tabasco to taste, then add the shrimp, cod, and monkfish. Cover and cook on high for 30 minutes, until the fish is cooked and the shrimp have changed color. Taste and adjust the seasoning if necessary and serve.

Bell peppers, tomatoes, chiles, garlic, and herbs give this seafood medley
a fabulous depth of flavor and a colorful appearance.

Southwestern Seafood Stew

Ingredients

2 tbsp olive oil, plus extra for drizzling

1 large onion, chopped

4 garlic cloves, finely chopped

1 yellow bell pepper, peeled, seeded,
    and chopped

1 red bell pepper, peeled, seeded,
    and chopped

1 orange bell pepper, peeled, seeded,
    and chopped

1 lb tomatoes, peeled and chopped

2 large, mild green chiles, such as
    poblano, chopped

finely grated rind and juice of 1 lime

2 tbsp chopped fresh cilantro, plus extra
    leaves to garnish

1 bay leaf

2 cups fish, vegetable, or chicken stock

1 lb red snapper

1 lb raw shrimp

8 oz cleaned squid

salt and pepper

⊙ Serves 4

🥣 Preparation time: 20 minutes,
    plus 15 minutes pre-cooking

🧤 Cooking time: 8 hours

---

1. Heat the oil in a pan. Add the onion and garlic and cook over low heat, stirring
occasionally, for 5 minutes, until softened. Add the bell peppers, tomatoes, and chiles
and cook, stirring frequently, for 5 minutes. Stir in the lime rind and juice, add the
cilantro and bay leaf, and pour in the stock. Bring to a boil, stirring occasionally.

2. Transfer the mixture to the slow cooker, cover, and cook on low for 7½ hours.
Meanwhile, skin the fish fillets, if necessary, and cut the flesh into chunks. Shell
and devein the shrimp. Cut the squid bodies into rings and halve the tentacles or
leave them whole.

3. Add the seafood to the stew, season with salt and pepper, re-cover, and cook on high
for 30 minutes, or until tender and cooked through. Remove and discard the bay leaf,
garnish the stew with coriander leaves, and serve.

This fabulous vegetarian dish, based on the new season's fresh, young vegetables, is guaranteed to become a favorite even among meat-eaters.

Spring Stew

Ingredients

2 tbsp olive oil

4–8 pearl onions, halved

2 celery stalks, cut into ¼-inch slices

8 oz young carrots, halved if large

11 oz new potatoes, halved

4–5 cups vegetable stock

1¼ cups dried cannellini beans, soaked overnight in cold water and drained

1 bouquet garni

1½–2 tbsp light soy sauce

¾ cup baby corn

⅔ cup shelled fava beans, thawed if frozen

2½ cups shredded Savoy cabbage

1½ tbsp cornstarch

salt and pepper

⅔–1 cup freshly grated Parmesan cheese, to serve

🍽 Serves 4

🥄 Preparation time: 15 minutes, plus overnight soaking, plus 10–12 minutes pre-cooking

🧤 Cooking time: 3¼–4¼ hours

---

1. Heat the oil in a pan. Add the onions, celery, carrots, and potatoes and cook over low heat, stirring frequently, for 5–8 minutes, until softened. Add the stock, cannellini beans, bouquet garni, and soy sauce, bring to a boil, then transfer to the slow cooker.

2. Add the corn, fava beans, and cabbage, season with salt and pepper, and stir well. Cover and cook on high for 3–4 hours, until the vegetables are tender.

3. Remove and discard the bouquet garni. Stir the cornstarch with 3 tbsp water to a paste in a small bowl, then stir into the stew. Re-cover and cook on high for a further 15 minutes, until thickened. Serve the stew with the Parmesan handed separately.

Entertaining

There is something almost magical about coming home on a cold day to a tender beef pot roast and all its accompanying vegetables.

Traditional Pot Roast

Ingredients

1 onion, finely chopped

4 carrots, sliced

4 baby turnips sliced

4 celery stalks, sliced

2 potatoes, peeled and sliced

1 sweet potato, peeled and sliced

3–4 lb beef pot roast

1 bouquet garni

1¼ cups boiling beef stock

salt and pepper

Serves 6

Preparation time: 20 minutes

Cooking time: 9–10 hours

1. Place the onion, carrots, turnips, celery, potatoes, and sweet potato in the slow cooker and stir to mix well.

2. Rub the beef all over with salt and pepper, then place on top of the bed of vegetables. Add the bouquet garni and pour in the stock. Cover and cook on low for 9–10 hours, until the beef is cooked to your liking.

3. Remove the beef, carve into slices, and arrange on serving plates. Spoon some of the vegetables and cooking juices onto the plates and serve.

As the duckling is braised gently, all the meat becomes deliciously tender, so you can use the whole bird for this tasty dish.

Duckling with Apples

Ingredients

4–4 lb 8 oz duckling, cut into 8 pieces

2 tbsp olive oil

1 onion, finely chopped

1 carrot, finely chopped

1¼ cups chicken stock

1¼ cups dry white wine

bouquet garni

¼ cup butter

4 eating apples

salt and pepper

Serves 4

Preparation time: 15 minutes, plus 15 minutes pre-cooking, plus 5 minutes to finish

Cooking time: 8 hours

1. Season the duckling pieces with salt and pepper. Heat the oil in a large, heavy skillet. Add all the duckling pieces, placing the breast portions skin side down. Cook over medium–high heat for a few minutes until golden brown, then transfer the breast portions to a plate. Turn the other pieces and continue to cook until browned all over. Transfer to the plate.

2. Add the onion and carrot to the skillet and cook over low heat, stirring occasionally, for 5 minutes until the onion is softened. Add the stock and wine and bring to a boil.

3. Transfer the vegetable mixture to the slow cooker. Add the duckling pieces and the bouquet garni. Cover and cook on low for 8 hours, occasionally skimming off the fat from the slow cooker and replacing the lid immediately each time.

4. Shortly before you are ready to serve, peel, core, and slice the apples. Melt the butter in a large skillet. Add the apple slices and cook over medium heat, turning occasionally, for 5 minutes until golden.

5. Spoon the cooked apples onto warmed plates and divide the duckling among them. Skim off the fat and strain the sauce into a pitcher, then pour it over the duckling, and serve.

This North African combination of lamb, dried fruit, and nuts is delicately spiced and wonderfully rich in flavor.

Lamb Tagine

Ingredients

3 tbsp olive oil

2 red onions, chopped

2 garlic cloves, finely chopped

1-inch piece fresh gingerroot, finely chopped

1 yellow bell pepper, seeded and chopped

2 lb 4 oz boneless shoulder of lamb,
   trimmed and cut into 1-inch cubes

3¾ cups lamb or chicken stock

1 cup no-soak dried apricots, halved

1 tbsp honey

4 tbsp lemon juice

pinch of saffron threads

2-inch cinnamon stick

salt and pepper

To garnish

½ cup sliced almonds, toasted

fresh cilantro sprigs

Serves 6

Preparation time: 15 minutes,
plus 10 minutes pre-cooking

Cooking time: 8½ hours

---

1. Heat the oil in a large, heavy pan. Add the onions, garlic, ginger, and bell pepper and cook over low heat, stirring occasionally, for 5 minutes until the onion has softened. Add the lamb and stir well to mix, then pour in the stock. Add the apricots, honey, lemon juice, saffron, and cinnamon stick, and season with the salt and pepper. Bring to a boil.

2. Transfer the mixture to the slow cooker. Cover and cook on low for 8½ hours until the meat is tender.

3. Remove and discard the cinnamon stick. Transfer to warmed serving bowls, sprinkle with the almonds, garnish with fresh cilantro, and serve.

Seasonal ingredients have a deliciously fresh flavor, but you can enjoy the taste of springtime at any time of year if you use frozen asparagus.

Springtime Lamb with Asparagus

Ingredients

2 tbsp sunflower oil

1 onion, thinly sliced

2 garlic cloves, very finely chopped

2 lb 4 oz boneless shoulder of lamb,
   cut into 1-inch cubes

8 oz asparagus spears, thawed if frozen

1¼ cups chicken stock

4 tbsp lemon juice

⅔ cup heavy cream

salt and pepper

Serves 6

Preparation time: 20 minutes,
plus 10 minutes pre-cooking,
plus 5 minutes to finish

Cooking time: 7¼ hours

1. Heat the oil in a large, heavy skillet. Add the onion and cook over medium heat, stirring occasionally, for 5 minutes until softened. Add the garlic and lamb and cook, stirring occasionally, for 5 minutes more until the lamb is lightly browned all over.

2. Meanwhile, trim off and reserve the tips of the asparagus spears. Cut the stalks into 2–3 pieces. Add the stock and lemon juice to the skillet, season with salt and pepper, and bring to a boil. Lower the heat, add the asparagus stalks, and simmer for 2 minutes.

3. Transfer the mixture to the slow cooker. Cover and cook on low for 7 hours until the lamb is tender.

4. About 20 minutes before you intend to serve, cook the reserved asparagus tips in a pan of lightly salted, boiling water for 5 minutes. Drain well, then combine with the cream. Spoon the cream mixture on top of the lamb mixture but do not stir it in. Re-cover and cook on high for 15–20 minutes to heat through before serving.

This is the perfect choice for slow cooking as the meat becomes melt-in-your-mouth tender and the flavors mingle superbly.

Lamb Shanks with Olives

Ingredients

1½ tbsp all-purpose flour

4 lamb shanks

2 tbsp olive oil

1 onion, sliced

2 garlic cloves, finely chopped

2 tsp sweet paprika

14 oz canned chopped tomatoes

2 tbsp tomato paste

2 carrots, sliced

2 tsp sugar

1 cup red wine

2-inch cinnamon stick

2 fresh rosemary sprigs

1 cup pitted black olives

2 tbsp lemon juice

2 tbsp chopped fresh mint

salt and pepper

fresh mint sprigs, to garnish

Serves 4

Preparation time: 15 minutes, plus 15 minutes pre-cooking

Cooking time: 8½ hours

---

1. Spread out the flour on a plate and season with salt and pepper. Toss the lamb in the seasoned flour and shake off any excess. Heat the oil in a large, heavy pan. Add the lamb shanks and cook over medium heat, turning frequently, for 6–8 minutes until browned all over. Transfer to a plate and set aside.

2. Add the onion and garlic to the pan and cook, stirring frequently, for 5 minutes until softened. Stir in the paprika and cook for 1 minute. Add the tomatoes, tomato paste, carrots, sugar, wine, cinnamon stick, and rosemary and bring to a boil.

3. Transfer the vegetable mixture to the slow cooker and add the lamb shanks. Cover and cook on low for 8 hours until the lamb is very tender.

4. Add the olives, lemon juice, and mint to the slow cooker. Re-cover and cook on high for 30 minutes. Remove and discard the rosemary and cinnamon and serve, garnished with mint sprigs.

Olives, chiles, capers, and, of course, almonds provide a delicious mix of flavors in this traditional Mexican stew.

Pork with Almonds

Ingredients

2 tbsp corn or sunflower oil

2 onions, chopped

2 garlic cloves, finely chopped

2-inch cinnamon stick

3 cloves

1 cup ground almonds

1 lb 10 oz boneless pork,
  cut into 1-inch cubes

4 tomatoes, peeled and chopped

2 tbsp capers

1 cup green olives, pitted

3 pickled jalapeño chiles, drained,
  seeded, and cut into rings

1½ cups chicken stock

salt and pepper

fresh cilantro sprigs, to garnish (optional)

Serves 4

Preparation time: 25 minutes,
plus 25 minutes pre-cooking

Cooking time: 5 hours

---

1. Heat half the oil in a large, heavy skillet. Add the onions and cook over low heat, stirring occasionally, for 5 minutes until softened. Add the garlic, cinnamon, cloves, and almonds and cook, stirring frequently, for 8–10 minutes. Be careful not to burn the almonds.

2. Remove and discard the spices and transfer the mixture to a food processor. Process to a smooth purée.

3. Rinse out the skillet and return to the heat. Heat the remaining oil, then add the pork, in batches if necessary. Cook over medium heat, stirring frequently, for 5–10 minutes until browned all over. Return all the pork to the skillet and add the almond purée, tomatoes, capers, olives, chiles, and chicken stock. Bring to a boil, then transfer to the slow cooker.

4. Season with salt and pepper and mix well. Cover and cook on low for 5 hours. To serve, transfer to warmed plates and garnish with cilantro sprigs, if desired.

Chicken simmers to tender perfection in a rich sauce flavored with walnuts, lemon, ginger, and, surprisingly, molasses.

Nutty Chicken

Ingredients

3 tbsp sunflower oil

4 skinless chicken portions

2 shallots, chopped

1 tsp ground ginger

1 tbsp all-purpose flour

scant 2 cups beef stock

½ cup walnut pieces

grated rind of 1 lemon

2 tbsp lemon juice

1 tbsp molasses

salt and pepper

fresh watercress or mizuna sprigs,
  to garnish

🍽 Serves 4

🥄 Preparation time: 15 minutes,
   plus 10–15 minutes pre-cooking

🧤 Cooking time: 6 hours

---

1. Heat the oil in a large, heavy skillet. Season the chicken portions with salt and pepper and add to the skillet. Cook over medium heat, turning occasionally, for 5–8 minutes, until lightly golden all over. Transfer to the slow cooker.

2. Add the shallots to the skillet and cook, stirring occasionally, for 3–4 minutes until softened. Sprinkle in the ginger and flour and cook, stirring constantly, for 1 minute. Gradually stir in the stock and bring to a boil, stirring constantly. Lower the heat and simmer for 1 minute, then stir in the nuts, lemon rind and juice, and molasses.

3. Pour the sauce over the chicken. Cover and cook on low for 6 hours until the chicken is cooked through and tender. Taste and adjust the seasoning if necessary. Transfer the chicken to warm bowls, spoon some of the sauce over each portion, garnish with watercress sprigs, and serve immediately.

This is a great way to cook a family-size piece of cured ham as it prevents the meat from drying out and lets the delicious spicy flavors penetrate.

Cured Ham Cooked in Cider

Ingredients

2 lb 4 oz boneless cured ham in a single piece

1 onion, halved

4 cloves

6 black peppercorns

1 tsp juniper berries

1 celery stalk, chopped

1 carrot, sliced

3 cups hard cider

fresh vegetables, such as mashed
    potatoes and peas, to serve

Serves 6

Preparation time: 10 minutes,
plus 15 minutes standing

Cooking time: 8 hours

1. Place a trivet or rack in the slow cooker, if you like, and stand the ham on it. Otherwise, just place the ham in the cooker. Stud each of the onion halves with 2 cloves and add to the cooker with the peppercorns, juniper berries, celery, and carrot.

2. Pour in the hard cider, cover, and cook on low for 8 hours until the meat is tender.

3. Remove the ham from the cooker and place on a board. Tent with foil and let stand for 10–15 minutes. Discard the cooking liquid and flavorings.

4. Cut off any rind and fat from the ham, then carve into slices, and serve with fresh vegetables.

Serve this traditional Italian dish with pasta, or a crisp mixed salad if you are following a low-carb diet.

Chicken Cacciatore

Ingredients

3 tbsp olive oil

4 chicken portions, skinned

2 onions, sliced

2 garlic cloves, finely chopped

14 oz canned chopped tomatoes

1 tbsp tomato paste

2 tbsp chopped fresh parsley

2 tsp fresh thyme leaves

⅔ cup red wine

salt and pepper

fresh thyme sprigs, to garnish

 Serves 4

Preparation time: 20 minutes, plus 15 minutes pre-cooking

Cooking time: 5 hours

1. Heat the oil in a heavy skillet. Add the chicken portions and cook over medium heat, turning occasionally, for 10 minutes until golden all over. Using a slotted spoon, transfer the chicken to the slow cooker.

2. Add the onions to the skillet and cook, stirring occasionally, for 5 minutes until softened and just turning golden. Add the garlic, tomatoes and their can juices, tomato paste, parsley, thyme, and wine. Season with salt and pepper and bring to a boil.

3. Pour the tomato mixture over the chicken pieces. Cover and cook on low for 5 hours until the chicken is tender and cooked through. Taste and adjust the seasoning if necessary, and serve, garnished with sprigs of thyme.

The musky, slightly honey flavor of this wine complements the chicken superbly and its steely edge cuts through the richness of the cream.

Chicken in Riesling

Ingredients

2 tbsp all-purpose flour

1 chicken, about 3 lb 8 oz, cut into 8 pieces

¼ cup butter

1 tbsp sunflower oil

4 shallots, finely chopped

12 white mushrooms, sliced

2 tbsp brandy

2¼ cups Riesling wine

generous 1 cup heavy cream

salt and pepper

chopped fresh flat-leaf parsley, to garnish

Serves 4–6

Preparation time: 20 minutes, plus 15 minutes pre-cooking, plus 5 minutes for the sauce

Cooking time: 5–6 hours

---

1. Put the flour in a shallow dish and season with salt and pepper. Toss the chicken pieces in the flour until well coated and shake off any excess. Heat half the butter with the oil in a heavy skillet. Add the chicken pieces and cook over medium–high heat, turning frequently, for 10 minutes, until golden all over. Using a slotted spoon, transfer them to a plate.

2. Pour off the fat from the skillet and wipe the base with paper towels. Melt the remaining butter. Add the shallots and mushrooms and cook over medium–high heat, stirring constantly, for 3 minutes, until the shallots are golden and the mushrooms lightly browned. Return the chicken to the skillet and remove it from the heat. Warm the brandy in a small ladle, ignite, and pour it over the chicken, shaking the skillet gently until the flames have died down.

3. Return the skillet to the heat and pour in the wine. Bring to a boil over low heat, scraping any sediment from the base of the skillet. Transfer to the slow cooker, cover, and cook on low for 5–6 hours, until the chicken is tender.

4. Transfer the chicken to a serving dish and keep warm. Skim off any fat from the surface of the cooking liquid and pour the liquid into a pan. Stir in the cream and bring just to a boil over low heat. Season to taste with salt and pepper and pour the sauce over the chicken. Sprinkle with chopped parsley and serve immediately.

Although thought of as a fatty meat, duckling can often be disappointingly dry but there's no fear of failure with this luscious and colorful stew.

Duck & Red Wine Stew

Ingredients

4 duckling portions, about 6 oz each

1 red onion, cut into wedges

2–3 garlic cloves, chopped

1 large carrot, chopped

2 celery stalks, chopped

2 tbsp all-purpose flour

1¼ cups red wine

2 tbsp brandy

¾ cup chicken stock or water

3-inch strip of thinly pared orange rind

2 tbsp red currant jelly

1½ cups sugar snap peas

1–2 tsp olive oil

4 oz white mushrooms

salt and pepper

1 tbsp chopped fresh parsley, to garnish

Serves 4

Preparation time: 10 minutes, plus 15 minutes pre-cooking

Cooking time: 8½ hours

---

1. Heat a heavy skillet for 1 minute, then add the duckling portions, and cook over low heat until the fat runs. Increase the heat to medium and cook, turning once, for 5 minutes, until browned on both sides. Using a slotted spoon, transfer to the slow cooker.

2. Add the onion, garlic, carrot, and celery to the skillet and cook, stirring occasionally, for 5 minutes, until softened. Sprinkle in the flour and cook, stirring constantly, for 2 minutes, then remove the skillet from the heat. Gradually stir in the wine, brandy, and stock, return the skillet to the heat, and bring to a boil, stirring constantly. Season with salt and pepper and stir in the orange rind and red currant jelly. Pour the mixture over the duckling portions, cover, and cook on low for 8 hours, occasionally skimming off the fat from the stew and replacing the lid of the slow cooker immediately each time.

3. Cook the sugar snaps in a pan of boiling water for 3 minutes, then drain. Heat the olive oil in another pan, add the mushrooms, and cook, stirring frequently for 3 minutes. Add the sugar snaps and mushrooms to the stew, re-cover, and cook on high for 25–30 minutes, until tender. Serve garnished with the parsley.

Venison, the name for meat from a wide variety of deer, is easy to obtain these days and usually less expensive than beef. It is tasty, nutritious, and low in fat.

 Venison Casserole

Ingredients

3 tbsp olive oil

2 lb 4 oz stewing venison,
cut into 1¼-inch cubes

2 onions, thinly sliced

2 garlic cloves, chopped

1½ cups beef stock

2 tbsp all-purpose flour

½ cup port

2 tbsp red currant jelly

6 juniper berries, crushed

4 cloves, crushed

pinch of ground cinnamon

pinch of freshly grated nutmeg

salt and pepper

mashed potatoes, to serve

Serves 6

Preparation time: 15 minutes,
plus 15 minutes pre-cooking

Cooking time: 7–8 hours

1. Heat the oil in a heavy skillet. Add the venison and cook over high heat, stirring frequently, for 5 minutes, until browned all over. Using a slotted spoon, transfer it to the slow cooker.

2. Add the onions and garlic to the skillet, lower the heat, and cook, stirring occasionally, for 5 minutes, until softened. Transfer them to the slow cooker.

3. Gradually stir the stock into the skillet, scraping up any sediment from the base, then bring to a boil, stirring constantly. Sprinkle the flour over the meat in the slow cooker and stir well to coat evenly. Stir in the hot stock, then stir in the port, red currant jelly, juniper berries, cloves, cinnamon, and nutmeg. Season with salt and pepper. Cover and cook on low for 7–8 hours, until the meat is tender.

4. Taste and adjust the seasoning if necessary. Remove and discard the cloves, then serve with mashed potatoes.

This elegant dish tastes fabulous and will be a sure-fire hit at any dinner party, yet it is surprisingly easy to prepare.

Seafood in Saffron Sauce

Ingredients

2 tbsp olive oil

1 onion, sliced

2 celery stalks, sliced

pinch of saffron threads

1 tbsp chopped fresh thyme

2 garlic cloves, finely chopped

1 lb 12 oz canned tomatoes,
   drained and chopped

¾ cup dry white wine

8¾ cups fish stock

8 oz live clams

8 oz live mussels

12 oz red snapper fillets

1 lb monkfish fillet

8 oz squid rings, thawed if frozen

2 tbsp shredded fresh basil leaves

salt and pepper

Serves 4

Preparation time: 10 minutes,
plus 10 minutes pre-cooking

Cooking time: 5½ hours

1. Heat the oil in a heavy skillet. Add the onion, celery, saffron, thyme, and a pinch of salt and cook over low heat, stirring occasionally, for 5 minutes, until softened. Add the garlic and cook, stirring constantly, for 2 minutes.

2. Add the tomatoes, wine, and stock, season with salt and pepper, and bring to a boil, stirring constantly. Transfer the mixture to the slow cooker, cover, and cook on low for 5 hours.

3. Meanwhile, scrub the shellfish under cold running water and pull the "beards" off the mussels. Discard any with broken shells or that do not shut immediately when sharply tapped. Cut the snapper and monkfish fillets into bite-size chunks.

4. Add the pieces of fish, the shellfish, and the squid rings to the slow cooker, re-cover, and cook on high for 30 minutes, until the clams and mussels have opened and the fish is cooked through. Discard any shellfish that remain closed. Stir in the basil and serve.

Inspired by the cuisine of Southeast Asia, this colorful and aromatic vegetarian medley would be a delightful treat for friends who don't eat meat.

Fragrant Vegetable Pot

Ingredients

3 tbsp peanut oil

9 oz firm tofu, cut into bite-size cubes

1-inch piece fresh gingerroot, grated

2 lemongrass stalks, finely chopped

1–2 garlic cloves, crushed

1–2 Thai chiles, seeded and chopped

3 celery stalks, sliced

3 shallots, cut into wedges

6 oz carrots, cut into batons

1 red bell pepper, seeded and cut into chunks

1 yellow bell pepper, seeded and cut into chunks

1 cup baby corn

1 tsp brown sugar

2½ cups vegetable stock

2 tbsp light soy sauce

1½ tbsp cornstarch

¾ cup green beans

3 oz head broccoli, divided into florets

6 scallions

1 tbsp chopped fresh cilantro

pepper

jasmine rice, to serve

🍽 Serves 4

🥄 Preparation time: 20 minutes, plus 20 minutes pre-cooking

🧤 Cooking time: 5¾–6 hours

---

1. Heat 2 tbsp of the oil in a heavy skillet. Add the tofu and cook over low heat, stirring frequently, for 8–10 minutes, until golden brown all over. Using a slotted spoon, transfer to a plate and set aside.

2. Drain and wipe the skillet with paper towels. Add the remaining oil and heat. Add the ginger, lemongrass, garlic, and chiles and cook over medium heat, stirring frequently, for 3 minutes. Add the celery and shallots and cook, stirring constantly, for 2 minutes, then add the carrots, bell peppers, and baby corn. Sprinkle with the sugar, stir in the stock and soy sauce, and bring to a boil, stirring. Transfer to the slow cooker, cover, and cook on low for 5 hours.

3. Stir the cornstarch with 3 tbsp water to a paste in a small bowl, then stir into the slow cooker. Add the beans, broccoli, scallions, cilantro, and tofu, season with pepper, and stir gently. Re-cover and cook on high for 45–60 minutes, until all the vegetables are tender. Serve with jasmine rice.

It's hard to believe that the humble bean stew could become so glamorous and tasty as this marvelous mingling of flavors and textures.

Bean Stew

Ingredients

1 large fennel bulb

2 tbsp olive oil

1 red onion, cut into small wedges

2–4 garlic cloves, sliced

1 green chile, seeded and chopped

1 eggplant, about 8 oz, cut into chunks

2 tbsp tomato paste

2 cups vegetable stock

1 lb tomatoes

1 tbsp balsamic vinegar

4 fresh oregano sprigs

14 oz canned borlotti beans,
  drained and rinsed

14 oz canned cannellini beans,
  drained and rinsed

1 yellow bell pepper, seeded and cut into
  small strips

1 zucchini, halved lengthwise and sliced

½ cup pitted black olives

salt and pepper

1 oz Parmesan cheese, to garnish

Serves 4

Preparation time: 20 minutes,
plus 15–20 minutes pre-cooking

Cooking time: 3–4 hours

---

1. Trim the fennel bulb, reserving the feathery fronds, then cut the bulb into thin strips. Heat the oil in a heavy skillet. Add the fennel strips, onion, garlic, and chile and cook over low heat, stirring occasionally, for 5–8 minutes, until softened. Add the eggplant and cook, stirring frequently, for 5 minutes.

2. Combine the tomato paste and half the stock in a pitcher and add to the skillet. Pour in the remaining stock, add the tomatoes, vinegar, and oregano, and bring to a boil, stirring constantly.

3. Transfer the mixture to the slow cooker. Stir in the beans, bell pepper, zucchini, and olives, and season with salt and pepper. Cover and cook on high for 3–4 hours, until all the vegetables are tender.

4. Taste and adjust the seasoning if necessary. Thinly shave the Parmesan over the top of the stew, garnish with the reserved fennel fronds, and serve.

Winter Warmers

This hearty, one-pot, vegetarian dish is simplicity itself, but if you're too tired to bother with the dumplings, just serve it with fresh crusty bread.

Vegetable Stew with Dumplings

Ingredients

½ rutabaga, cut into chunks

2 onions, sliced

2 potatoes, cut into chunks

2 carrots, cut into chunks

2 celery stalks, sliced

2 zucchini, sliced

2 tbsp tomato paste

2½ cups hot vegetable stock

1 bay leaf

1 tsp ground coriander

½ tsp dried thyme

14 oz canned corn, drained

salt and pepper

For the parsley dumplings

1¾ cups self-rising flour

⅔ cup vegetable shortening

2 tbsp chopped fresh parsley

½ cup milk

Serves 6

Preparation time: 20 minutes

Cooking time: 6½ hours

1. Put the rutabaga, onions, potatoes, carrots, celery, and zucchini into the slow cooker. Stir the tomato paste into the stock and pour it over the vegetables. Add the bay leaf, coriander, and thyme and season with salt and pepper. Cover and cook on low for 6 hours.

2. To make the dumplings, sift the flour with a pinch of salt into a bowl and stir in the shortening and parsley. Add just enough milk to make a firm but light dough. Knead lightly and shape into 12 small balls.

3. Stir the corn into the vegetable stew and place the dumplings on top. Cook on high for 30 minutes. Serve immediately.

Chipotle chiles are smoked jalapeños and they impart a distinctive flavor to this dish, but remember that they are still hot.

Chipotle Chicken

Ingredients

4–6 dried chipotle chiles

4 garlic cloves, unpeeled

1 small onion, chopped

14 oz canned chopped tomatoes

1¼ cups boiling chicken or vegetable stock

4 skinless chicken breast portions

salt and pepper

Serves 4

Preparation time: 10 minutes, plus 30 minutes soaking, plus 5–10 minutes to finish

Cooking time: 5 hours

1. Preheat the oven to 400°F. Place the chiles in a bowl and pour in just enough hot water to cover. Set aside to soak for 30 minutes. Meanwhile, place the unpeeled garlic cloves on a cookie sheet and roast in the oven for about 10 minutes until soft. Remove from the oven and let cool.

2. Drain the chiles, reserving ½ cup of the soaking water. Seed the chiles, if you like, and chop coarsely. Place the chiles and reserved soaking water in a blender or food processor and process to a purée. Peel and mash the garlic in a bowl.

3. Place the chile purée, garlic, onion, and tomatoes in the slow cooker and stir in the stock. Season the chicken portions with salt and pepper and place them in the slow cooker. Cover and cook on low for about 5 hours until the chicken is tender and cooked through.

4. Lift the chicken out of the slow cooker with a slotted spoon, cover, and keep warm. Pour the cooking liquid into a pan and bring to a boil on the stove. Boil for 5–10 minutes until reduced. Place the chicken on warmed plates, spoon the sauce over it, and serve.

This makes a great vegetarian main course, but also goes well with lean roast meat, such as chicken.

Winter Vegetable Medley

Ingredients

2 tbsp sunflower oil

2 onions, chopped

3 carrots, chopped

3 parsnips, chopped

2 bunches celery, chopped, leaves reserved

2 tbsp chopped fresh parsley

1 tbsp chopped fresh cilantro

1¼ cups vegetable stock

salt and pepper

Serves 4

Preparation time: 15 minutes, plus 10 minutes pre-cooking

Cooking time: 3 hours

---

1. Heat the oil in a large, heavy pan. Add the onions and cook over medium heat, stirring occasionally, for 5 minutes until softened. Add the carrots, parsnips, and celery and cook, stirring occasionally, for 5 minutes more. Stir in the herbs, season with salt and pepper, and pour in the stock. Bring to a boil.

2. Transfer the vegetable mixture to the slow cooker, cover, and cook on high for 3 hours until tender. Taste and adjust the seasoning if necessary. Using a slotted spoon, transfer the medley to warmed plates, then spoon over a little of the cooking liquid. Garnish with a few of the reserved celery leaves.

Hot pepper sauce is the key ingredient to the flavor of this spicy dish, but you can adjust the amount so you choose just how fiery you want it to be.

Pepper Pot-style Stew

Ingredients

1½ tbsp all-purpose flour

1 lb braising beef, cut into 1-inch cubes

2 tbsp olive oil

1 red onion, sliced

3–4 garlic cloves, crushed

1 green chile, seeded and chopped

3 celery stalks, sliced

4 cloves

1 tsp ground allspice

1–2 tsp hot pepper sauce

2½ cups beef stock

1¾ cups chopped peeled acorn or other squash

1 large red bell pepper, seeded and chopped

4 tomatoes, coarsely chopped

4 oz okra, trimmed and halved

mixed wild and long-grain rice, to serve

Serves 4

Preparation time: 20 minutes, plus 15 minutes pre-cooking

Cooking time: 9 hours

1. Spread out the flour in a shallow dish, add the steak cubes, and toss until well coated. Shake off any excess and reserve the remaining flour.

2. Heat the oil in a heavy skillet. Add the onion, garlic, chile, celery, cloves, and allspice and cook over low heat, stirring occasionally, for 5 minutes, until the vegetables have softened. Increase the heat to high, add the steak cubes, and cook, stirring frequently, for 3 minutes, until browned all over. Sprinkle in the reserved flour and cook, stirring constantly, for 2 minutes, then remove the skillet from the heat.

3. Stir in the hot pepper sauce, then gradually stir in the stock. Return the skillet to the heat and bring to a boil, stirring constantly. Transfer the mixture to the slow cooker and add the squash. Cover and cook on low for 8 hours.

4. Add the bell pepper, tomatoes, and okra, re-cover, and cook on high for 1 hour. Serve with mixed wild and long-grain rice.

This substantial one-pot dish is terrific served on its own, with boiled rice or with crusty bread—whichever way, it will certainly keep out winter's chill.

Vegetable & Lentil Casserole

Ingredients

1 onion

10 cloves

1 cup green lentils

1 bay leaf

6¾ cups boiling vegetable stock

2 leeks, sliced

2 potatoes, diced

2 carrots, chopped

3 zucchini, sliced

1 celery stalk, sliced

1 red bell pepper, seeded and chopped

1 tbsp lemon juice

salt and pepper

Serves 4

Preparation time: 10 minutes

Cooking time: 4½–6 hours

---

1. Peel the onion, stud it with the cloves and place it in the slow cooker. Add the lentils and bay leaf, pour in the stock, cover, and cook on high for 1½–2 hours.

2. Remove the onion with a slotted spoon and re-cover the slow cooker. Remove and discard the cloves and slice the onion. Add the onion, leeks, potatoes, carrots, zucchini, celery, and bell pepper to the lentils, season with salt and pepper, re-cover, and cook on high for 3–4 hours, until all the vegetables are tender.

3. Remove and discard the bay leaf and stir in the lemon juice. Taste and adjust the seasoning if necessary, then serve.

Just the aroma and appearance of this colorful dish—a fusion of European and North African cuisines—will make the family feel cozy on a freezing winter day.

Pork & Vegetable Ragout

Ingredients

1 lb lean, boneless pork

1½ tbsp all-purpose flour

1 tsp ground coriander

1 tsp ground cumin

1½ tsp ground cinnamon

1 tbsp olive oil

1 onion, chopped

14 oz canned chopped tomatoes

2 tbsp tomato paste

1¼ cups chicken stock

1¼ cups chopped carrots

2⅔ cups chopped squash, such as kabocha

2 cups sliced leeks, blanched and drained

4 oz okra, trimmed and sliced

salt and pepper

fresh parsley sprigs, to garnish

couscous, to serve

Serves 4

Preparation time: 20 minutes, plus 18–20 minutes pre-cooking

Cooking time: 5–6 hours

1. Trim off any visible fat from the pork and cut the flesh into thin strips about 2 inches long. Combine the flour, coriander, cumin, and cinnamon in a shallow dish, add the pork strips, and toss well to coat. Shake off the excess and reserve the remaining spiced flour.

2. Heat the oil in a heavy skillet. Add the onion and cook over low heat, stirring occasionally, for 5 minutes, until softened. Add the pork strips, increase the heat to high, and cook, stirring frequently, for 5 minutes, until browned all over. Sprinkle in the reserved spiced flour and cook, stirring constantly, for 2 minutes, then remove the skillet from the heat.

3. Gradually stir in the tomatoes with their can juices. Combine the tomato paste with the stock in a pitcher, then gradually stir the mixture into the skillet. Add the carrots, return the skillet to the heat, and bring to a boil, stirring constantly.

4. Transfer to the slow cooker, stir in the squash, leeks, and okra, and season with salt and pepper. Cover and cook on low for 5–6 hours, until the meat and vegetables are tender. Garnish with parsley sprigs and serve with couscous.

Not only is this mildly spiced dish great for family meals, it is also special enough to serve to guests at an informal dinner party.

Cinnamon Lamb Casserole

Ingredients

2 tbsp all-purpose flour

2 lb 4 oz lean boneless lamb, cubed

2 tbsp olive oil

2 large onions, sliced

1 garlic clove, finely chopped

1¼ cups red wine

2 tbsp red wine vinegar

14 oz canned chopped tomatoes

scant ½ cup raisins

1 tbsp ground cinnamon

pinch of sugar

1 bay leaf

salt and pepper

To garnish

⅔ cup plain strained yogurt

2 garlic cloves, crushed

paprika, for sprinkling

Serves 6

Preparation time: 15 minutes, plus 15 minutes pre-cooking

Cooking time: 8–8½ hours

1. Spread out the flour in a shallow dish and season with pepper. Add the lamb cubes and toss until well coated, shaking off any excess.

2. Heat the oil in a heavy skillet. Add the onions and garlic and cook over low heat, stirring occasionally, for 5 minutes, until softened. Increase the heat to high, add the lamb, and cook, stirring frequently, for 5 minutes, until evenly browned.

3. Stir in the wine, vinegar, and tomatoes with their can juices, and bring to a boil, scraping up any sediment from the base of the skillet. Transfer to the slow cooker, stir in the raisins, cinnamon, sugar, and bay leaf, and season with salt and pepper. Cover and cook on low for 8–8½ hours, until the lamb is tender.

4. Meanwhile, prepare the garnish. Combine the yogurt and garlic in a small bowl and season to taste with salt and pepper. Cover and chill in the refrigerator until ready to serve.

5. Remove and discard the bay leaf. Serve each portion topped with a spoonful of the garlic-flavored yogurt sprinkled with a little paprika.

This is a wonderfully adaptable recipe that can be served with other Indian dishes or simply with plain boiled rice.

Vegetable Curry

Ingredients

2 tbsp vegetable oil

1 tsp cumin seeds

1 onion, sliced

2 curry leaves

1-inch piece fresh gingerroot,
    finely chopped

2 fresh red chiles, seeded and chopped

2 tbsp curry paste

2 carrots, sliced

1½ cups snow peas

1 head cauliflower, cut into florets

3 tomatoes, peeled and chopped

¾ cup frozen peas, thawed

½ tsp ground turmeric

⅔–1 cup boiling vegetable or chicken stock

salt and pepper

Serves 4–6

Preparation time: 15 minutes,
plus 20 minutes pre-cooking

Cooking time: 5 hours

---

1. Heat the oil in a large, heavy pan. Add the cumin seeds and cook, stirring constantly, for 1–2 minutes until they give off their aroma and begin to pop. Add the onion and curry leaves and cook, stirring occasionally, for 5 minutes until the onion has softened. Add the ginger and chiles and cook, stirring occasionally, for 1 minute.

2. Stir in the curry paste and cook, stirring, for 2 minutes, then add the carrots, snow peas, and cauliflower florets. Cook for 5 minutes, then add the tomatoes, peas, and turmeric, and season with salt and pepper. Cook for 3 minutes, then add ⅔ cup of the stock, and bring to a boil.

3. Transfer the mixture to the slow cooker. If the vegetables are not covered, add more hot stock, then cover, and cook on low for 5 hours until tender. Remove and discard the curry leaves before serving.

Four kinds of beans, a medley of vegetables, and of course, chiles are combined in this vibrant and delicious vegetarian main course.

Chili Bean Stew

Ingredients

2 tbsp olive oil

1 onion, chopped

2–4 garlic cloves, chopped

2 red chiles, seeded and chopped

1⅔ cups drained canned red kidney beans, rinsed

1⅓ cups drained canned garbanzo beans, rinsed

1⅔ cups drained canned cannellini beans, rinsed

1 tbsp tomato paste

3 cups vegetable stock

1 red bell pepper, seeded and chopped

4 tomatoes, coarsely chopped

generous 1 cup shelled fava beans, thawed if frozen

1 tbsp chopped fresh cilantro

sour cream, to serve

To garnish

fresh cilantro sprigs

pinch of paprika

Serves 4–6

Preparation time: 15 minutes, plus 10 minutes pre-cooking

Cooking time: 4–4½ hours

---

1. Heat the oil in a heavy skillet. Add the onion, garlic, and chiles and cook over low heat, stirring occasionally, for 5 minutes, until softened. Add the kidney beans, garbanzo beans, and cannellini beans. Combine the tomato paste with a little of the stock in a pitcher and pour it over the beans. Add the remaining stock and bring to a boil.

2. Transfer the mixture to the slow cooker, cover, and cook on low for 3 hours. Stir in the bell pepper, tomatoes, fava beans, and chopped cilantro, re-cover, and cook on high for 1–1½ hours, until all the beans are tender.

3. Serve the stew topped with spoonfuls of sour cream and garnished with cilantro sprigs and a sprinkling of paprika.

This colorful dish makes an economical and tasty midweek supper when served with boiled rice.

Mixed Bean Chili

Ingredients

2 tbsp corn oil

1 onion, chopped

1 garlic clove, finely chopped

1 fresh red chile, seeded and chopped

1 yellow bell pepper, seeded and chopped

1 tsp ground cumin

1 tbsp chili powder

⅔ cup dried red kidney beans, soaked overnight, drained, and rinsed

⅔ cup dried black beans, soaked overnight, drained, and rinsed

⅔ cup dried pinto beans, soaked overnight, drained, and rinsed

4 cups vegetable stock

1 tbsp sugar

salt and pepper

chopped fresh cilantro, to garnish

Serves 4–6

Preparation time: 10 minutes, plus overnight soaking, plus 25 minutes pre-cooking

Cooking time: 10 hours

---

1. Heat the oil in a large, heavy pan. Add the onion, garlic, chile, and bell pepper and cook over medium heat, stirring occasionally, for 5 minutes. Stir in the cumin and chili powder and cook, stirring, for 1–2 minutes. Add the drained beans and stock and bring to a boil. Boil vigorously for 15 minutes.

2. Transfer the mixture to the slow cooker, cover, and cook on low for 10 hours until the beans are tender.

3. Season the mixture with salt and pepper, then ladle about one-third into a bowl. Mash well with a potato masher, then return the mashed beans to the cooker, and stir in the sugar. Serve immediately, sprinkled with chopped fresh cilantro.

Cook's tip

Both kidney beans and black beans contain a toxin (pinto beans don't) that is destroyed by vigorous boiling. It is important, therefore, that they are pre-cooked before being transferred to the slow cooker.

This is an inexpensive and easy dish—plus it is very good on a cold evening.

Sausage & Bean Stew

Ingredients

2 tbsp sunflower oil

2 onions, chopped

2 garlic cloves, finely chopped

⅔ cup chopped bacon

1 lb 2 oz pork sausage links

14 oz canned navy beans, red kidney beans, or black-eyed peas, drained and rinsed

2 tbsp chopped fresh parsley

⅔ cup boiling beef stock

To serve

4 slices French bread

½ cup grated Swiss cheese

Serves 4

Preparation time: 10 minutes, plus 10 minutes pre-cooking

Cooking time: 6 hours

---

1. Heat the oil in a heavy skillet. Add the onions and cook over low heat, stirring occasionally, for 5 minutes until softened. Add the garlic, bacon, and sausage links, and cook, stirring and turning the sausages occasionally, for 5 minutes more.

2. Using a slotted spoon, transfer the mixture from the skillet to the slow cooker. Add the beans, parsley, and beef stock, then cover, and cook on low for 6 hours.

3. Just before serving, lightly toast the bread under a preheated broiler. Divide the grated cheese among the toast slices and place under the broiler until just melted.

4. Ladle the stew onto warmed plates, top each portion with the cheese-toast, and serve.

While this is certainly not a traditional recipe, this vegetarian version is filling, nourishing, and packed with flavor.

Vegetable Goulash

Ingredients

¼ cup chopped sun-dried tomatoes

2 tbsp olive oil

½–1 tsp crushed dried chiles

2–3 garlic cloves, chopped

1 large onion, cut into small wedges

1 small celery root, cut into small chunks

8 oz carrots, sliced

8 oz new potatoes, cut into chunks

1¾ cups chopped acorn squash

2 tbsp tomato paste

1¼ cups vegetable stock

1 cup green lentils

1–2 tsp hot paprika

3 fresh thyme sprigs, plus extra to garnish

1 lb tomatoes

sour cream, to serve

Serves 4

Preparation time: 20 minutes, plus 15–20 minutes soaking, plus 10–12 minutes pre-cooking

Cooking time: 5¼ hours

---

1. Put the sun-dried tomatoes in a small heatproof bowl, add freshly boiled water to cover, and let soak for 15–20 minutes.

2. Heat the oil in a heavy pan. Add the chiles, garlic, onion, celery root, carrots, potatoes, and squash and cook over medium–low heat, stirring frequently, for 5–8 minutes, until softened. Combine the tomato paste with the stock in a pitcher and stir it into the pan. Add the lentils, sun-dried tomatoes with their soaking liquid, the paprika, and thyme and bring to a boil.

3. Transfer the mixture to the slow cooker, cover, and cook on low for 4½ hours. Add the tomatoes, re-cover, and cook on high for 45 minutes, until all the vegetables and lentils are tender. Remove and discard the thyme sprigs. Serve the goulash topped with sour cream and garnished with extra thyme sprigs.

This is a great dish to serve at an informal dinner party, with plenty of salad and fresh crusty bread for mopping up the tasty juices.

Duckling Jambalaya-style Stew

Ingredients

4 duckling breasts, about 6 oz each

2 tbsp olive oil

1⅓ cups diced cured ham

8 oz chorizo or other spicy sausages,
   skinned and sliced

1 onion, chopped

3 garlic cloves, chopped

3 celery stalks, chopped

1–2 red chiles, seeded and chopped

1 green bell pepper, seeded and chopped

2½ cups chicken stock

1 tbsp chopped fresh oregano

14 oz canned chopped tomatoes

1–2 tsp hot pepper sauce

fresh parsley sprigs, to garnish

To serve

salad greens

boiled rice

Serves 4

Preparation time: 15 minutes,
plus 12–15 minutes pre-cooking

Cooking time: 6 hours

---

1. Remove and discard the skin and any visible fat from the duckling breasts and cut the flesh into bite-size pieces. Heat half the oil in a heavy skillet, add the duckling, ham, and chorizo, and cook over high heat, stirring frequently, for 5 minutes, until browned all over. Using a slotted spoon, transfer the meat to the slow cooker.

2. Add the onion, garlic, celery, and chiles to the skillet, lower the heat, and cook, stirring occasionally, for 5 minutes, until softened. Add the bell pepper and stir in the stock, oregano, tomatoes with the can juices, and hot pepper sauce. Bring to a boil, then pour the mixture over the meat.

3. Cover the slow cooker and cook on low for 6 hours, until the meat is tender. Serve garnished with parsley sprigs and accompanied by salad greens and boiled rice.

This is a great dish for informal entertaining as long as your guests don't mind its being slightly messy to eat. Finger bowls are essential.

Shellfish Stew

Ingredients

1 tbsp olive oil

⅔ cup diced bacon

2 tbsp butter

2 shallots, chopped

2 leeks, sliced

2 celery stalks, chopped

2 potatoes, diced

1 lb 8 oz tomatoes, peeled, seeded, and chopped

3 tbsp chopped fresh parsley

3 tbsp snipped fresh chives, plus extra to garnish

1 bay leaf

1 fresh thyme sprig

6¼ cups fish stock

24 live mussels

24 live clams

1 lb porgy fillets

24 raw jumbo shrimp

salt and pepper

Serves 8

Preparation time: 20 minutes, plus 20 minutes pre-cooking

Cooking time: 7½ hours

1. Heat the oil in a heavy skillet. Add the bacon and cook, stirring frequently, for 5–8 minutes, until crisp. Using a slotted spoon, transfer to the slow cooker. Add the butter to the skillet and when it has melted, add the shallots, leeks, celery, and potatoes. Cook over low heat, stirring occasionally, for 5 minutes, until softened. Stir in the tomatoes, parsley, chives, bay leaf, and thyme, pour in the stock, and bring to a boil, stirring constantly. Pour the mixture into the slow cooker, cover, and cook on low for 7 hours.

2. Meanwhile, scrub the mussels and clams under cold running water and pull off the "beards" from the mussels. Discard any with broken shells or that do not shut immediately when sharply tapped. Cut the fish fillets into bite-size chunks. Peel and devein the shrimp.

3. Remove and discard the bay leaf and thyme sprig from the stew. Season with salt and pepper and add all the seafood. Re-cover and cook on high for 30 minutes. Serve garnished with extra chives.

Around the World

This dish has been a national favorite for almost as long as the United States has existed and shows how New World ingredients gave new vitality to Old World cooking.

Brunswick Stew

Ingredients

4 lb chicken portions

2 tbsp paprika

2 tbsp olive oil

2 tbsp butter

1 lb onions, chopped

2 yellow bell peppers, seeded and chopped

14 oz canned chopped tomatoes

1 cup dry white wine

2 cups chicken stock

1 tbsp Worcestershire sauce

½ tsp Tabasco sauce

1 tbsp finely chopped fresh parsley

2 tbsp all-purpose flour

11½ oz canned corn, drained

15 oz canned lima beans, drained and rinsed

salt

fresh parsley sprigs, to garnish

Serves 6

Preparation time: 15 minutes, plus 20 minutes pre-cooking

Cooking time: 5½ hours

1. Season the chicken portions with salt and dust with the paprika. Heat the oil and butter in a heavy skillet. Add the chicken portions and cook over medium–high heat, turning frequently, for 10 minutes, until golden brown all over. Using a slotted spoon, transfer the chicken to the slow cooker.

2. Add the onions and bell peppers to the skillet, lower the heat, and cook, stirring occasionally, for 5 minutes, until softened. Add the tomatoes with their can juices, wine, stock, Worcestershire sauce, Tabasco sauce and chopped parsley and bring to a boil, stirring constantly. Pour the mixture over the chicken, cover, and cook on low for 5 hours.

3. Combine the flour and 4 tbsp water to a paste in a small, heatproof bowl. Add a ladleful of the cooking liquid and mix well, then stir the mixture into the stew. Add the corn and lima beans, re-cover, and cook on high for 30 minutes, until the chicken is tender and cooked through. Serve garnished with parsley sprigs.

Pork is traditionally served with sharp-flavored fruit to counterbalance its richness. This unusual and refreshing recipe uses pineapple to do this.

Mexican Pork Chops

Ingredients

4 pork chops, trimmed of excess fat

2 tbsp corn oil

1 lb canned pineapple cubes in fruit juice

1 red bell pepper, seeded and
   finely chopped

2 fresh jalapeño chiles, seeded and
   finely chopped

1 onion, finely chopped

1 tbsp chopped fresh cilantro

½ cup boiling chicken stock

salt and pepper

fresh cilantro sprigs, to garnish

tortillas, to serve

Serves 4

Preparation time: 15 minutes,
plus 10 minutes pre-cooking

Cooking time: 6¼ hours

---

1. Season the chops with salt and pepper. Heat the oil in a large, heavy skillet. Add the chops and cook over medium heat for 2–3 minutes each side until lightly browned. Transfer them to the slow cooker. Drain the pineapple, reserving the juice, and set aside.

2. Add the bell pepper, chiles, and onion to the skillet and cook, stirring occasionally, for 5 minutes until the onion is softened. Transfer the mixture to the slow cooker and add the cilantro and stock, together with ½ cup of the reserved pineapple juice. Cover and cook on low for 6 hours until the chops are tender.

3. Add the reserved pineapple to the slow cooker, re-cover, and cook on high for 15 minutes. Garnish with fresh cilantro sprigs and serve immediately, with tortillas.

This summery dish from the Sunshine State is sure to bring a smile to the faces of your guests or family whatever time of year you serve it.

Florida Chicken

Ingredients

1½ tbsp all-purpose flour

1 lb skinless, boneless chicken, cut into
   bite-size pieces

1 tbsp olive oil

1 onion, cut into wedges

2 celery stalks, sliced

⅔ cup orange juice

1¼ cups chicken stock

1 tbsp light soy sauce

1–2 tsp honey

1 tbsp grated orange rind

1 orange bell pepper, seeded and chopped

8 oz zucchini, halved lengthwise and
   sliced

2 corn cobs

1 orange, peeled and segmented

salt and pepper

1 tbsp chopped fresh parsley, to garnish

Serves 4

Preparation time: 15 minutes,
plus 15 minutes pre-cooking

Cooking time: 5¼ hours

---

1. Spread out the flour in a shallow dish and season with salt and pepper. Add the chicken and toss well to coat, shaking off any excess. Reserve the remaining seasoned flour.

2. Heat the oil in a heavy skillet. Add the chicken and cook over high heat, stirring frequently, for 5 minutes, until golden brown all over. Using a slotted spoon, transfer the chicken to the slow cooker.

3. Add the onion and celery to the skillet, lower the heat and cook, stirring occasionally, for 5 minutes, until softened. Sprinkle in the reserved seasoned flour and cook, stirring constantly, for 2 minutes. Remove the skillet from the heat. Gradually stir in the orange juice, stock, soy sauce, and honey, then add the orange rind. Return the skillet to the heat and bring to a boil, stirring constantly.

4. Pour the mixture over the chicken and add the bell pepper, zucchini, and corn cobs. Cover and cook on low for 5 hours, until the chicken is tender and cooked through. Stir in the orange, re-cover, and cook on high for 15 minutes. Serve garnished with the parsley.

Packed with flavor and bursting with color, this is a perfect dish to come home to after a busy day.

Caribbean Beef Stew

Ingredients

1 lb braising beef

3½ cups diced pumpkin or other squash

1 onion, chopped

1 red bell pepper, seeded and chopped

2 garlic cloves, finely chopped

1-inch piece fresh gingerroot, finely chopped

1 tbsp sweet or hot paprika

1 cup beef stock

14 oz canned chopped tomatoes

14 oz canned pigeon peas, drained and rinsed

14 oz canned black-eyed peas,
    drained and rinsed

salt and pepper

Serves 6

Preparation time: 20 minutes,
plus 10 minutes pre-cooking

Cooking time: 7½ hours

1. Trim off any visible fat from the beef, then dice the meat. Heat a large, heavy pan without adding any extra fat. Add the meat and cook, stirring constantly, for a few minutes until browned all over. Stir in the pumpkin, onion, and bell pepper and cook for 1 minute, then add the paprika, stock, and tomatoes, and bring to a boil.

2. Transfer the mixture to the slow cooker, cover, and cook on low for 7 hours. Add the pigeon peas and black-eyed peas to the stew and season to taste with salt and pepper. Re-cover and cook on high for 30 minutes, then serve.

This Louisiana classic is thought to get its name from the French jambon or the Spanish jamón—meaning ham, which is a traditional ingredient.

Jambalaya

Ingredients

½ tsp cayenne pepper

½ tsp freshly ground black pepper

1 tsp salt

2 tsp chopped fresh thyme

12 oz skinless, boneless
   chicken breasts, diced

2 tbsp corn oil

2 onions, chopped

2 garlic cloves, finely chopped

2 green bell peppers, seeded and chopped

2 celery stalks, chopped

⅔ cup chopped smoked ham

generous 1 cup sliced chorizo sausage

14 oz canned chopped tomatoes

2 tbsp tomato paste

1 cup chicken stock

1 lb peeled raw shrimp

2⅔ cups cooked rice

snipped fresh chives, to garnish

Serves 6

Preparation time: 20 minutes,
plus 15 minutes pre-cooking

Cooking time: 6½ hours

---

1. Combine the cayenne, black pepper, salt, and thyme in a bowl. Add the chicken and toss to coat. Heat the oil in a large, heavy pan. Add the onions, garlic, bell peppers, and celery and cook over low heat, stirring occasionally, for 5 minutes. Add the chicken and cook over medium heat, stirring frequently, for 5 minutes more until golden all over. Stir in the ham, chorizo, tomatoes, tomato paste, and stock and bring to a boil.

2. Transfer the mixture to the slow cooker. Cover and cook on low for 6 hours. Add the shrimp and rice, re-cover, and cook on high for 30 minutes.

3. Taste and adjust the seasoning, if necessary. Transfer to warm plates, garnish with chives, and serve the jambalaya immediately.

It is well worth buying a full-bodied, good-quality red wine—preferably Burgundy—for this perennially popular French classic.

Boeuf Bourguignonne

Ingredients

1 cup diced bacon

2 tbsp all-purpose flour

2 lb braising beef, trimmed and
   cut into 1-inch cubes

3 tbsp olive oil

2 tbsp butter

12 pearl onions or shallots

2 garlic cloves, finely chopped

⅔ cup beef stock

2 cups full-bodied red wine

bouquet garni

2 cups sliced mushrooms

salt and pepper

|O| Serves 6

Preparation time: 15 minutes,
plus 15 minutes pre-cooking

Cooking time: 7¼ hours

---

1. Cook the bacon in a large, heavy pan, stirring occasionally, until the fat runs and the pieces are crisp. Meanwhile, spread out the flour on a plate and season with salt and pepper. Toss the steak cubes in the flour to coat, shaking off any excess. Using a slotted spoon, transfer the bacon to a plate. Add the oil to the pan. When it is hot, add the steak cubes and cook, in batches, stirring occasionally, for 5 minutes until browned all over. Transfer to the plate with a slotted spoon.

2. Add the butter to the pan. When it has melted, add the onions and garlic and cook, stirring occasionally, for 5 minutes. Return the bacon and steak to the pan and pour in the stock and wine. Bring to a boil.

3. Transfer the mixture to the slow cooker and add the bouquet garni. Cover and cook on low for 7 hours until the meat is tender.

4. Add the mushrooms to the slow cooker and stir well. Re-cover and cook on high for 15 minutes.

5. Remove and discard the bouquet garni. Adjust the seasoning if necessary, then serve immediately.

All French coastal regions have their own specialty fish stew. Packed with the flavors of the Mediterranean, this is undoubtedly one of the most delicious.

French-style Fish Stew

Ingredients

large pinch of saffron threads
2 lb mixed white fish, such as sea
   bass, monkfish, red snapper,
   and grouper, filleted
24 raw jumbo shrimp
1 cleaned squid
2 tbsp olive oil
1 large onion, finely chopped
1 fennel bulb, thinly sliced,
   feathery fronds reserved
2 large garlic cloves, crushed
4 tbsp Pernod
4 cups fish stock

2 large tomatoes, peeled, seeded,
   and diced, or 14 oz canned chopped
   tomatoes, drained
1 tbsp tomato paste
1 bay leaf
pinch of sugar
pinch of dried chile flakes (optional)
salt and pepper

Serves 4–6

Preparation time: 25 minutes,
plus 10–12 minutes pre-cooking

Cooking time: 6½ hours

---

1. Toast the saffron threads in a small, dry skillet over high heat, stirring constantly, for 1 minute, until they give off their aroma. Tip into a bowl and set aside. Cut the fish fillets into large chunks. Peel and devein the shrimp, reserving the heads and shells. Cut off and reserve the tentacles from the squid and slice the body into ¼-inch rings. Place the seafood in a bowl, cover, and chill in the refrigerator until required. Tie the heads and shells of the shrimp in a piece of cheesecloth.

2. Heat the oil in a heavy skillet. Add the onion and fennel and cook over low heat, stirring occasionally, for 5 minutes, until softened. Add the garlic and cook, stirring frequently, for 2 minutes. Remove the skillet from the heat. Heat the Pernod in a ladle or small saucepan, ignite, and pour it over the onion and fennel, gently shaking the skillet until the flames have died down.

3. Return the skillet to the heat, stir in the toasted saffron, stock, tomatoes, tomato paste, bay leaf, sugar, and chile flakes, if using, and season with salt and pepper. Bring to a boil, then transfer to the slow cooker, add the bag of shrimp shells, cover and cook on low for 6 hours.

4. Remove and discard the bag of shrimp shells and the bay leaf. Add the seafood to the slow cooker, cover, and cook on high for 30 minutes, until the fish flakes easily with the point of a knife. Serve garnished with the reserved fennel fronds.

This is only one, although perhaps the most famous, of Mediterranean fish soups. For the best flavor, it should include a variety of different fish.

Bouillabaisse

Ingredients

5 lb mixed white fish, such as red snapper, porgy, sea bass, monkfish and whiting, filleted and bones and heads reserved, if possible
1 lb raw shrimp
grated rind of 1 orange
pinch of saffron threads
4 garlic cloves, finely chopped
1 cup olive oil
2 onions, finely chopped
1 leek, thinly sliced
4 potatoes, thinly sliced
2 large tomatoes, peeled and chopped

1 bunch fresh flat-leaf parsley, chopped
1 fresh fennel sprig
1 fresh thyme sprig
1 bay leaf
2 cloves
6 black peppercorns
1 strip orange rind
sea salt
crusty bread or croutons, to serve

Serves 6

Preparation time: 45 minutes

Cooking time: 8½ hours

---

1. Cut the fish fillets into bitesized pieces and peel and devein the shrimp. Reserve the heads and shells of the shrimp. Rinse the fish bones, if using, and cut off the gills of any fish heads. Place the chunks of fish and the shrimp in a large bowl. Sprinkle with the grated orange rind, saffron, half the garlic, and 2 tablespoons of the oil. Cover and set aside in the refrigerator.

2. Put the remaining garlic, the onions, leek, potatoes, tomatoes, parsley, fennel, thyme, bay leaf, cloves, peppercorns, and strip of orange rind in the slow cooker. Add the fish heads and bones, if using, and the shrimp shells and heads. Pour in the remaining olive oil and 12½ cups boiling water or enough to cover the ingredients by 1 inch. Season with sea salt. Cover and cook on low for 8 hours.

3. Strain the stock and return the liquid to the slow cooker. Discard the flavorings, fish and shrimp trimmings but retain the vegetables and return them to the slow cooker if you like. Add the fish and shrimp mixture, re-cover, and cook on high for 30 minutes until the fish is cooked through and flakes easily with the point of a knife.

4. Ladle into warmed bowls and serve with crusty bread or croutons.

This fabulous combination of sweet and savory, refreshing and warming flavors is typical of the Maghreb—the area of North Africa that includes Algeria, Morocco, and Tunisia.

Mediterranean Lamb with Apricots & Pistachios

Ingredients

pinch of saffron threads

1 lb boneless lamb leg steaks

1½ tbsp all-purpose flour

1 tsp ground coriander

½ tsp ground cumin

½ tsp ground allspice

1 tbsp olive oil

1 onion, chopped

2–3 garlic cloves, chopped

2 cups lamb or chicken stock

1 cinnamon stick

scant ½ cup chopped dried apricots

1⅓ cups sliced zucchini

4 oz cherry tomatoes

1 tbsp chopped fresh cilantro

salt and pepper

2 tbsp coarsely chopped pistachios, to garnish

couscous or rice, to serve

Serves 4

Preparation time: 20 minutes, plus 15 minutes pre-cooking

Cooking time: 8 hours

1. Put the saffron threads in a small heatproof bowl, add 2 tbsp freshly boiled water, and let steep for 10 minutes. Meanwhile, trim off any visible fat from the lamb steaks and cut the flesh into 1-inch chunks. Combine the flour, coriander, cumin, and allspice in a shallow dish, add the lamb, and toss until well coated, shaking off any excess. Reserve the remaining spiced flour.

2. Heat the oil in a heavy skillet. Add the onion and garlic and cook over low heat, stirring occasionally, for 5 minutes, until softened. Add the pieces of lamb, increase the heat to high, and cook, stirring frequently, for 3 minutes, until browned on all sides. Sprinkle in the reserved spiced flour and cook, stirring constantly, for 2 minutes, then remove the skillet from the heat.

3. Gradually stir in the stock and the saffron with its soaking liquid. Return the skillet to the heat and bring to a boil, stirring constantly. Transfer the mixture to the slow cooker and add the cinnamon stick, apricots, zucchini, and tomatoes. Cover and cook on low for 8 hours, until the meat is tender.

4. Remove and discard the cinnamon stick. Stir in the cilantro, season to taste with salt and pepper, sprinkle with the pistachios, and serve with couscous or rice.

This colorful vegetarian sauce is a little like the classic French dish ratatouille but has an extra tang of balsamic vinegar and lemon juice.

Sweet-and-Sour Sicilian Pasta

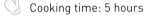

Ingredients

4 tbsp olive oil

1 large red onion, sliced

2 garlic cloves, finely chopped

2 red bell peppers, seeded and sliced

2 zucchini, cut into batons

1 eggplant, cut into batons

2 cups bottled strained tomatoes

4 tbsp lemon juice

2 tbsp balsamic vinegar

½ cup pitted black olives, sliced

1 tbsp sugar

14 oz dried fettucine or pappardelle

salt and pepper

fresh flat-leaf parsley sprigs, to garnish

Serves 4

Preparation time: 15 minutes, plus 15 minutes pre-cooking

Cooking time: 5 hours

---

1. Heat the oil in a large, heavy pan. Add the onion, garlic, and bell peppers and cook over low heat, stirring occasionally, for 5 minutes. Add the zucchini and eggplant and cook, stirring occasionally, for 5 minutes more. Stir in the strained tomatoes and ⅔ cup water and bring to a boil. Stir in the lemon juice, vinegar, olives, and sugar and season with salt and pepper.

2. Transfer the mixture to the slow cooker. Cover and cook on low for 5 hours until all the vegetables are tender.

3. To cook the pasta, bring a large pan of lightly salted water to a boil. Add the fettuccine and bring back to a boil. Cook for 10–12 minutes until the pasta is tender but still firm to the bite. Drain and transfer to a warmed serving dish. Spoon the vegetable mixture over the pasta, toss lightly, garnish with parsley, and serve.

This is a classically simple dish that relies on using the best-quality ingredients in a complementary combination, all delicately flavored with thyme.

Chicken Italian Style

Ingredients

1 tbsp all-purpose flour

4 chicken portions, about 6 oz each

2½ tbsp olive oil

8–12 shallots, halved if large

2–4 garlic cloves, sliced

1¾ cups chicken stock

¼ cup dry sherry

4 fresh thyme sprigs

4 oz cherry tomatoes

1 cup baby corn, halved lengthwise

2 slices white or whole-wheat bread, crusts removed

salt and pepper

1 tbsp chopped fresh thyme, to garnish

Serves 4

Preparation time: 10 minutes, plus 20 minutes pre-cooking

Cooking time: 5–6 hours

---

1. Spread out the flour in a shallow dish and season with salt and pepper. Add the chicken portions and toss well to coat, shaking off any excess. Reserve the remaining seasoned flour.

2. Heat 1 tbsp of the oil in a heavy skillet. Add the chicken portions and cook over medium–high heat, turning frequently, for 10 minutes, until golden brown all over. Using a slotted spoon, transfer the chicken to the slow cooker.

3. Add the shallots and garlic to the skillet, lower the heat, and cook, stirring occasionally, for 5 minutes, until softened. Sprinkle in the reserved seasoned flour and cook, stirring constantly, for 2 minutes. Remove the skillet from the heat and gradually stir in the stock and sherry. Return the skillet to the heat and bring to a boil, stirring constantly.

4. Pour the mixture over the chicken and add the thyme sprigs, tomatoes, and baby corn. Cover and cook on low for 5–6 hours, until the chicken is tender and cooked through.

5. Meanwhile, cut the bread into cubes. Heat the remaining oil in a skillet, add the bread cubes, and cook, stirring frequently, for 4–5 minutes, until golden all over. Remove and discard the thyme sprigs from the stew, then serve, garnished with the croutons and chopped thyme.

Most regions of Italy boast of their stufato—slow-braised beef—and, hardly surprisingly, in Naples the recipe includes tomatoes.

Neapolitan Beef

Ingredients

1¼ cups red wine	3 lb 5 oz beef pot roast
4 tbsp olive oil	1–2 garlic cloves, thinly sliced
1 celery stalk, chopped	⅓ cup chopped bacon or pancetta
2 shallots, sliced	14 oz canned chopped tomatoes
4 garlic cloves, finely chopped	2 tbsp tomato paste
1 bay leaf	salt and pepper
10 fresh basil leaves, plus extra to garnish	
3 fresh parsley sprigs	Serves 6
pinch of grated nutmeg	Preparation time: 15 minutes, plus 12 hours marinating, plus 15 minutes pre-cooking
pinch of ground cinnamon	
2 cloves	Cooking time: 9 hours

1. Combine the wine, 2 tablespoons of the olive oil, the celery, shallots, garlic, herbs, and spices in a large, nonmetallic bowl. Add the beef, cover, and marinate, turning occasionally, for 12 hours.

2. Drain the beef, reserving the marinade, and pat dry with paper towels. Make small incisions all over the beef using a sharp knife. Insert a slice of garlic and a piece of bacon in each "pocket." Heat the remaining oil in a large skillet. Add the meat and cook over medium heat, turning frequently, until browned all over. Transfer the beef to the slow cooker.

3. Strain the reserved marinade into the skillet and bring to a boil. Stir in the tomatoes and tomato paste. Stir well, then pour the mixture over the beef. Cover and cook on low for about 9 hours until tender. If possible, turn the beef over halfway through the cooking time and re-cover the slow cooker immediately. To serve, remove the beef and place on a carving board. Cover with foil and let stand for 10–15 minutes to firm up. Cut into slices and transfer to a platter. Spoon the sauce over it and serve immediately.

Delicate North African spices complement the delicious flavor of this attractive fish which is usually cooked whole.

Moroccan Sea Bass

Ingredients

2 tbsp olive oil

2 onions, chopped

2 garlic cloves, finely chopped

2 carrots, finely chopped

1 fennel bulb, finely chopped

½ tsp ground cumin

½ tsp ground cloves

1 tsp ground coriander

pinch of saffron threads

1¼ cups fish stock

1 preserved or fresh lemon

2-lb sea bass, cleaned

salt and pepper

Serves 2

Preparation time: 15 minutes, plus 10 minutes pre-cooking, plus 5 minutes to finish

Cooking time: 6½–6¾ hours

---

1. Heat the oil in a large, heavy pan. Add the onions, garlic, carrots, and fennel and cook over medium heat, stirring occasionally, for 5 minutes. Stir in all the spices and cook, stirring, for 2 minutes more. Pour in the stock, season with salt and pepper, and bring to a boil.

2. Transfer the mixture to the slow cooker. Cover and cook on low for 6 hours or until the vegetables are tender.

3. Rinse the preserved lemon if using. Discard the fish head if you like. Slice the lemon and place the slices in the fish cavity, then place the fish in the slow cooker. Re-cover and cook on high for 30–45 minutes until the flesh flakes easily with the point of a knife.

4. Carefully transfer the fish to a platter and spoon the vegetables around it. Cover and keep warm. Transfer the cooking liquid to a pan and boil for a few minutes until reduced. Spoon it over the fish and serve.

This is a great main course dish for vegetarians and can also be served as an accompaniment to roast lamb or baked fish.

Moroccan Vegetable Stew

Ingredients

4 tomatoes, peeled, seeded, and chopped

3 cups vegetable stock

1 onion, sliced

2 carrots, diagonally sliced

1 tbsp chopped fresh cilantro

1⅓ cups sliced zucchini

1 small turnip, cubed

15 oz canned garbanzo beans,
   drained and rinsed

½ tsp ground turmeric

¼ tsp ground ginger

¼ tsp ground cinnamon

1⅓ cups couscous

salt

fresh cilantro sprigs, to garnish

Serves 4

Preparation time: 15 minutes,
plus 10 minutes pre-cooking

Cooking time: 3 hours

1. Put half the tomatoes in a blender or food processor and process until smooth. Scrape into a pan, add 2 cups of the stock, and bring to a boil. Pour the mixture into the slow cooker, add the remaining tomatoes, the onion, carrots, cilantro, zucchini, turnip, garbanzos, turmeric, ginger, and cinnamon, and stir well. Cover and cook on high for 3 hours.

2. Just before serving, bring the remaining stock to a boil in a large pan. Add a pinch of salt and sprinkle in the couscous, stirring constantly. Remove the pan from the heat, cover, and let stand for 5 minutes.

3. Fluff up the grains of couscous with a fork and divide it among 4 plates. Top with the vegetable stew, garnish with cilantro sprigs, and serve.

East meets West in Bulgarian cuisine, as typified by the combination of sweet paprika and hot chile in this classic dish.

Bulgarian Chicken

Ingredients

4 tbsp sunflower oil

6 chicken portions

2 onions, chopped

2 garlic cloves, finely chopped

1 fresh red chile, seeded and finely chopped

6 tomatoes, peeled and chopped

2 tsp sweet paprika

1 bay leaf

1 cup boiling chicken stock

salt and pepper

fresh thyme sprigs, to garnish (optional)

Serves 6

Preparation time: 20 minutes, plus 10 minutes pre-cooking

Cooking time: 6 hours

1. Heat half the oil in a large, heavy skillet. Add the chicken portions and cook over medium heat, turning occasionally, for about 10 minutes, until golden all over.

2. Transfer the contents of the skillet to the slow cooker and add the onions, garlic, chile, and tomatoes. Sprinkle in the paprika, add the bay leaf, and pour in the stock. Season with salt and pepper. Stir well, cover, and cook on low for 6 hours until the chicken is cooked through and tender. Remove and discard the bay leaf, then serve immediately.

This is simplicity itself, requiring very little preparation, yet it is packed with flavor and makes a great midweek supper. Serve with rice for a more substantial dish.

Easy Chinese Chicken

Ingredients

2 tsp grated fresh gingerroot

4 garlic cloves, finely chopped

2 star anise

⅔ cup Chinese rice wine or
   medium dry sherry

2 tbsp dark soy sauce

1 tsp sesame oil

4 skinless chicken thighs or drumsticks

shredded scallions, to garnish

Serves 4

Preparation time: 10 minutes,
plus 5 minutes pre-cooking

Cooking time: 4 hours

---

1. Combine the ginger, garlic, star anise, rice wine, soy sauce, and sesame oil in a bowl and stir in 5 tablespoons of water. Place the chicken in a pan, add the spice mixture, and bring to a boil.

2. Transfer to the slow cooker, cover, and cook on low for 4 hours, or until the chicken is tender and cooked through.

3. Remove and discard the star anise. Transfer the chicken to warmed plates and serve garnished with shredded scallions.

Contrasting flavors, colors, and textures make this tasty and attractive dish a perennial favorite among adults and children alike.

Pork Oriental

Ingredients

1 lb lean boneless pork

1½ tbsp all-purpose flour

1–2 tbsp peanut oil

1 onion, cut into small wedges

2–3 garlic cloves, chopped

1-inch piece fresh gingerroot, grated

1 red bell pepper, seeded and sliced

1 green bell pepper, seeded and sliced

1 tbsp tomato paste

1¼ cups chicken stock

8 oz canned pineapple chunks in
   natural juice

1–1½ tbsp dark soy sauce

1½ tbsp rice vinegar

4 scallions, diagonally sliced, to garnish

Serves 4

Preparation time: 15 minutes,
plus 15 minutes pre-cooking

Cooking time: 5½–6½ hours

---

1. Trim off all visible fat from the pork and cut the flesh into 1-inch chunks. Spread out the flour in a shallow dish, add the pork, and toss well to coat, shaking off any excess. Reserve the remaining flour.

2. Heat the oil in a heavy skillet. Add the onion, garlic, ginger, and bell peppers and cook over low heat, stirring occasionally, for 5 minutes, until softened. Add the pork, increase the heat, and cook, stirring frequently, for 5 minutes, until browned all over. Sprinkle in the reserved flour and cook, stirring constantly, for 2 minutes, then remove the skillet from the heat.

3. Combine the tomato paste with the stock in a pitcher, then gradually stir into the skillet. Drain the pineapple, reserving the juice. Stir the juice and soy sauce into the skillet. Return the skillet to the heat and bring to a boil, stirring constantly. Transfer to the slow cooker, cover, and cook on low for 5–6 hours.

4. Stir in the pineapple and vinegar, re-cover, and cook on high for 30 minutes. Serve garnished with the sliced scallions.

Desserts

This deliciously tangy dessert is a good, old-fashioned family favorite that looks and smells tempting and tastes scrumptious.

Magic Lemon Sponge

Ingredients

¾ cup superfine sugar

3 eggs, separated

1¼ cups milk

3 tbsp self-rising flour, sifted

⅔ cup freshly squeezed lemon juice

confectioners' sugar, for dusting

Serves 4

Preparation time: 20 minutes

Cooking time: 2½ hours

1. Beat the sugar with the egg yolks in a bowl, using an electric mixer. Gradually beat in the milk, followed by the flour and the lemon juice.

2. Whisk the egg whites in a separate, grease-free bowl until stiff. Fold half the whites into the yolk mixture using a rubber or plastic spatula in a figure-eight movement, then fold in the remainder. Try not to knock out the air.

3. Pour the mixture into an ovenproof dish, cover with foil, and place in the slow cooker. Add sufficient boiling water to come about one-third of the way up the side of the dish. Cover and cook on high for 2½ hours until the mixture has set and the sauce and sponge have separated.

4. Lift the dish out of the cooker and discard the foil. Lightly sift a little confectioners' sugar over the top and serve.

Served hot or cold, on its own or accompanied by cream, yogurt, or ice cream, this is always a sure-fire family favorite.

Apple Crumble

Ingredients

½ cup all-purpose flour

½ cup rolled oats

⅔ cup brown sugar

½ tsp grated nutmeg

½ tsp ground cinnamon

1 cup butter, softened

4 cooking apples, peeled, cored, and sliced

4–5 tbsp apple juice

Serves 4

Preparation time: 15 minutes

Cooking time: 5½ hours

---

1. Sift the flour into a bowl and stir in the oats, sugar, nutmeg, and cinnamon. Add the butter and mix in with a pastry blender or the prongs of a fork.

2. Place the apple slices in the base of the slow cooker and add the apple juice. Sprinkle the flour mixture evenly over them.

3. Cover and cook on low for 5½ hours. Serve hot, warm, or cold.

This rich, creamy rice dessert is a really comforting treat on cold winter days. You can serve it with canned or stewed fruit if you like.

Rice Pudding

Ingredients

⅔ cup short-grain rice

4 cups milk

generous ½ cup sugar

1 tsp vanilla extract

To decorate

ground cinnamon

4 cinnamon sticks

○| Serves 4

Preparation time: 5 minutes, plus 15–20 minutes pre-cooking

Cooking time: 2 hours

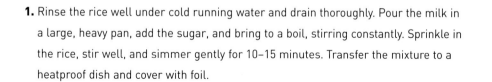

1. Rinse the rice well under cold running water and drain thoroughly. Pour the milk in a large, heavy pan, add the sugar, and bring to a boil, stirring constantly. Sprinkle in the rice, stir well, and simmer gently for 10–15 minutes. Transfer the mixture to a heatproof dish and cover with foil.

2. Place the dish in the slow cooker and add boiling water to come about one-third of the way up the side. Cover and cook on high for 2 hours.

3. Remove the dish from the slow cooker and discard the foil. Stir the vanilla extract into the rice, then spoon it into heatproof glasses or bowls. Dust lightly with ground cinnamon and decorate with cinnamon sticks.

This easy, yet very appealing dessert is great for dinner parties but not really suitable for serving to children.

Blushing Pears

Ingredients

6 small ripe pears

1 cup ruby port

1 cup superfine sugar

1 tsp finely chopped candied ginger

2 tbsp lemon juice

whipped cream or strained plain yogurt,
    to serve

Serves 6

Preparation time: 15 minutes,
plus cooling and chilling

Cooking time: 4 hours

1. Peel the pears, cut them in half lengthwise, and scoop out the cores. Place them in the slow cooker.

2. Combine the port, sugar, ginger, and lemon juice in a pitcher and pour the mixture over the pears. Cover and cook on low for 4 hours until the pears are tender.

3. Leave the pears to cool in the slow cooker, then carefully transfer to a bowl, and chill in the refrigerator until required.

4. To serve, partially cut each pear half into about 6 slices lengthwise, leaving the fruit intact at the stalk end. Carefully lift the pear halves onto serving plates and press gently to fan out the slices. Serve with whipped cream or yogurt.

This is a sophisticated version of the popular pudding using panettone, a light-textured Italian Christmas cake flavored with citrus rind and golden raisins.

Italian Bread Pudding

Ingredients

butter, for greasing

6 slices panettone

3 tbsp Marsala wine

1¼ cups milk

1¼ cups light cream

½ cup superfine sugar

grated rind of ½ lemon

pinch of ground cinnamon

3 extra large eggs, lightly beaten

heavy cream, to serve

Serves 6

Preparation time: 20 minutes, plus cooling and chilling

Cooking time: 2½ hours

1. Grease a heatproof bowl and set aside. Place the panettone on a deep plate and sprinkle with the Marsala wine.

2. Pour the milk and cream into a pan and add the sugar, lemon rind, and cinnamon. Gradually bring to a boil over low heat, stirring until the sugar has dissolved. Remove the pan from the heat and let cool slightly, then pour the mixture onto the eggs, beating constantly.

3. Place the panettone in the prepared bowl, pour in the egg mixture and cover with foil. Place in the slow cooker and add enough boiling water to come about one-third of the way up the side of the bowl. Cover and cook on high for 2½ hours until set.

4. Remove the bowl from the slow cooker and discard the foil. Let cool, then chill in the refrigerator until required. Loosen the sides of the pudding with a knife and turn out onto a serving dish. Serve with cream on the side.

index